ΛNTHEM

STRONG ALONE, STRONGER TOGETHER

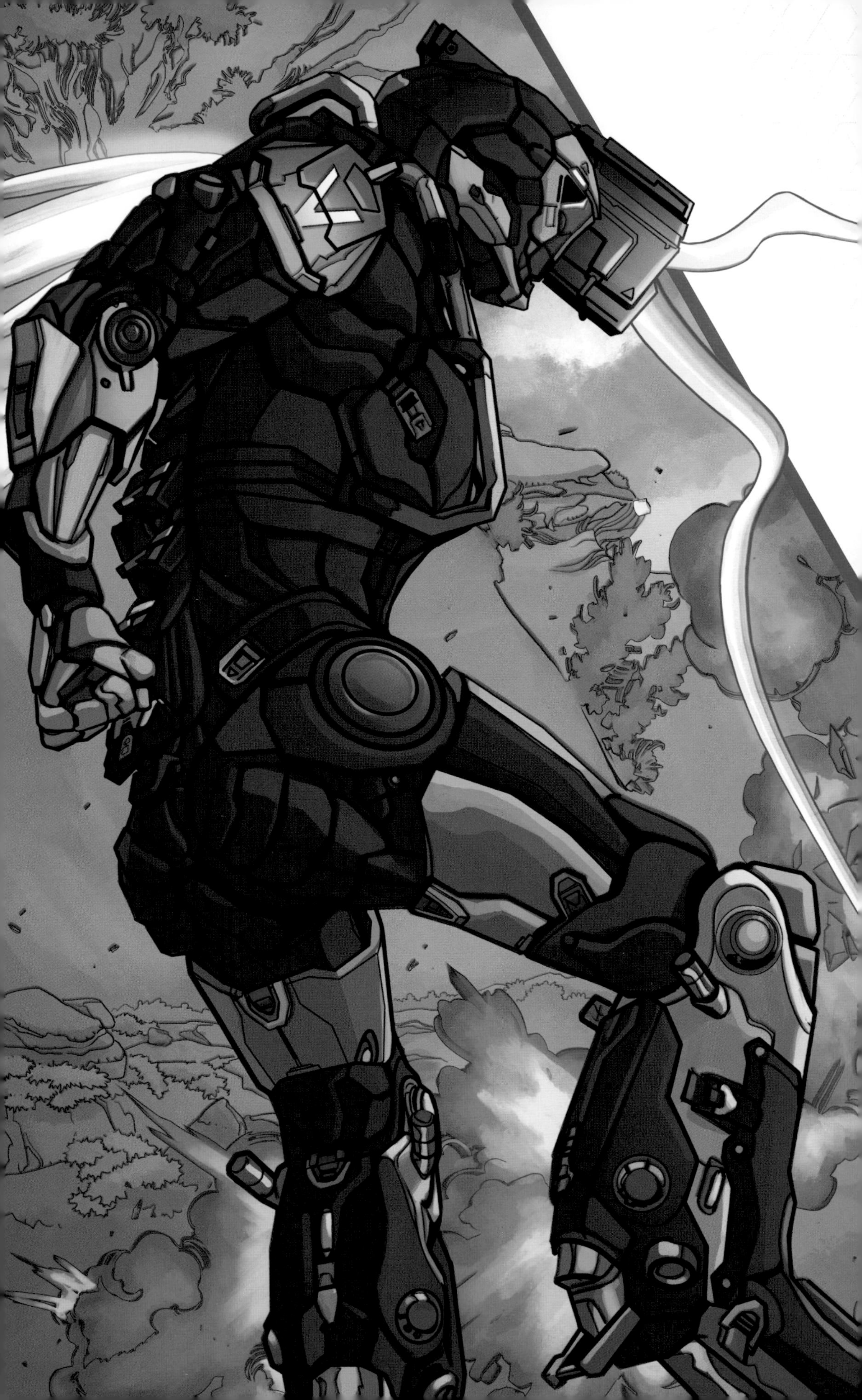

ANTHEM™

STRONG ALONE, STRONGER TOGETHER

STORY
MAC WALTERS AND **ALEXANDER FREED**

SCRIPT
ALEXANDER FREED

ART
EDUARDO FRANCISCO

COLORS
MICHAEL ATIYEH

LETTERING
**RICHARD STARKINGS &
COMICRAFT'S JIMMY BETANCOURT**

Dark Horse Books

PUBLISHER MIKE RICHARDSON
EDITOR DAVE MARSHALL
ASSISTANT EDITOR KONNER KNUDSEN
DESIGNER BRENNAN THOME
DIGITAL ART TECHNICIAN ALLYSON HALLER

Neil Hankerson Executive Vice President Tom Weddle Chief Financial Officer Randy Stradley Vice
President of Publishing Nick McWhorter Chief Business Development Officer Dale LaFountain
Chief Information Officer Matt Parkinson Vice President of Marketing Cara Niece Vice President
of Production and Scheduling Mark Bernardi Vice President of Book Trade and Digital Sales Ken
Lizzi General Counsel Dave Marshall Editor in Chief Davey Estrada Editorial Director Chris Warner
Senior Books Editor Cary Grazzini Director of Print and Development Lia Ribacchi Art Director
Vanessa Todd-Holmes Director of Print Purchasing Matt Dryer Director of Digital Art and Prepress
Michael Gombos Director of International Publishing and Licensing Kari Yadro Director of Custom
Programs Kari Torson Director of International Licensing Sean Brice Director of Trade Sales

Advertising Sales: (503) 905-2315 | ComicShopLocator.com

Special thanks to BioWare, including:
Derek Watts, Art Director | Chris Bain, Director of Business Development |
Casey Hudson, General Manager

ANTHEM: STRONG ALONE, STRONGER TOGETHER

This volume collects issues #1 through #3 of the Dark Horse comic-book series *Anthem*.

Published by Dark Horse Books
A division of Dark Horse Comics LLC
10956 SE Main Street
Milwaukie, OR 97222

darkhorse.com /// anthemthegame.com /// bioware.com

First Edition: August 2019
ISBN 978-1-50670-707-5
Digital ISBN 978-1-50670-709-9

10 9 8 7 6 5 4 3 2 1
Printed in China

Library of Congress Cataloging-in-Publication Data

Names: Walters, Mac, author. | Freed, Alexander, author. | Francisco, Edu,
    artist. | Atiyeh, Michael, colourist. | Starkings, Richard, letterer. |
    Betancourt, Jimmy, letterer.
Title: Anthem : strong alone, stronger together / story, Mac Walters and
    Alexander Freed ; script, Alexander Freed ; art, Eduardo Francisco ;
    colors, Michael Atiyeh ; lettering, Richard Starkings & Comicraft's Jimmy
    Betancourt.
Description: Milwaukie, OR : Dark Horse Books, 2019. | "This volume collects
    issues #1 through #3 of the Dark Horse comic-book series Anthem."
Identifiers: LCCN 2019009153 | ISBN 9781506707075 (hardback)
Subjects: LCSH: Graphic novels. | BISAC: COMICS & GRAPHIC NOVELS / Media
    Tie-In. | GAMES / Video & Electronic. | COMICS & GRAPHIC NOVELS / Science
    Fiction.
Classification: LCC PN6728.A65 W38 2019 | DDC 741.5/973--dc23
LC record available at https://lccn.loc.gov/2019009153

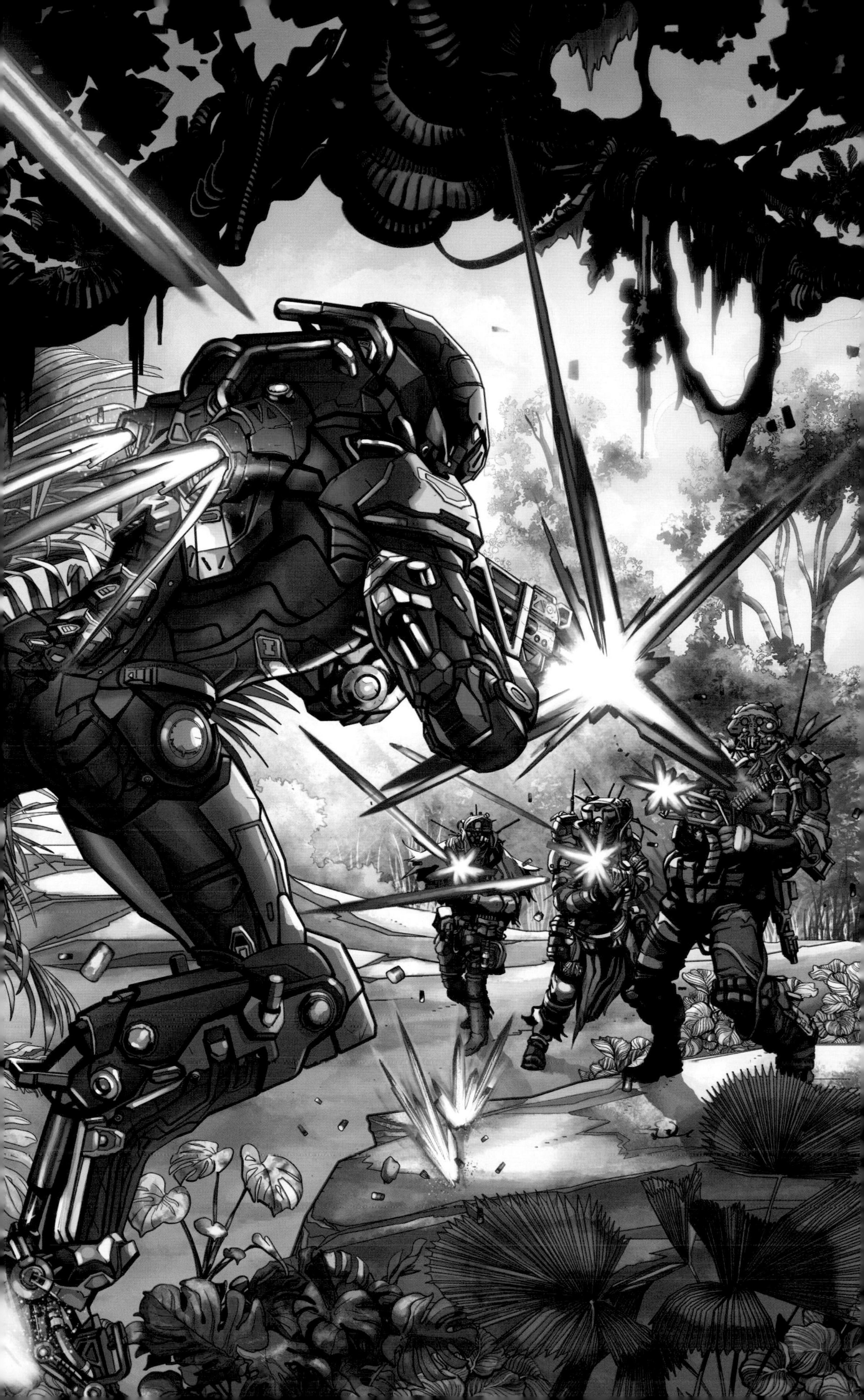

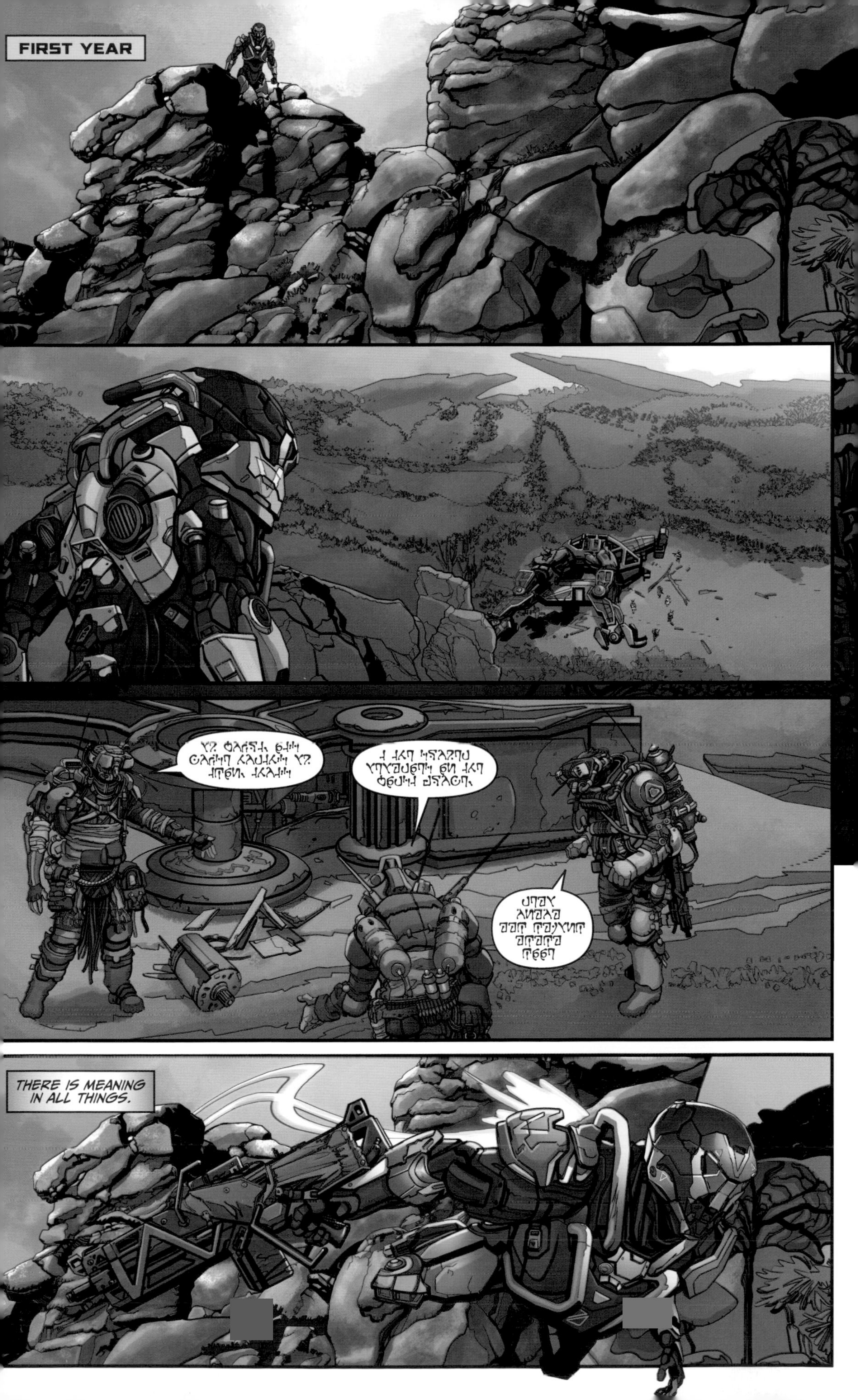
FIRST YEAR
THERE IS MEANING IN ALL THINGS.

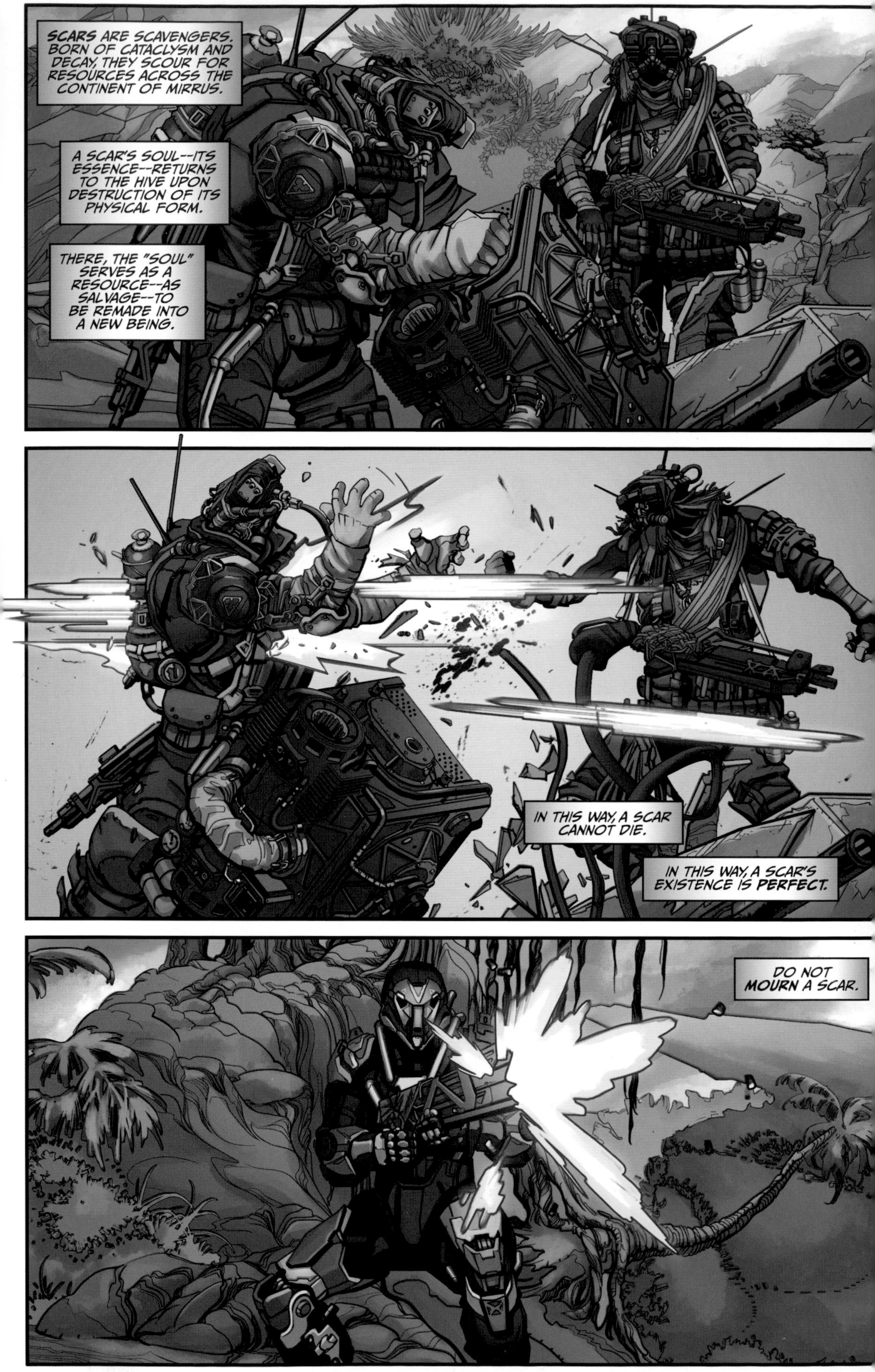
SCARS ARE SCAVENGERS. BORN OF CATACLYSM AND DECAY, THEY SCOUR FOR RESOURCES ACROSS THE CONTINENT OF MIRRUS.
A SCAR'S SOUL--ITS ESSENCE--RETURNS TO THE HIVE UPON DESTRUCTION OF ITS PHYSICAL FORM.
THERE, THE "SOUL" SERVES AS A RESOURCE--AS SALVAGE--TO BE REMADE INTO A NEW BEING.
IN THIS WAY, A SCAR CANNOT DIE.
IN THIS WAY, A SCAR'S EXISTENCE IS PERFECT.
DO NOT MOURN A SCAR.

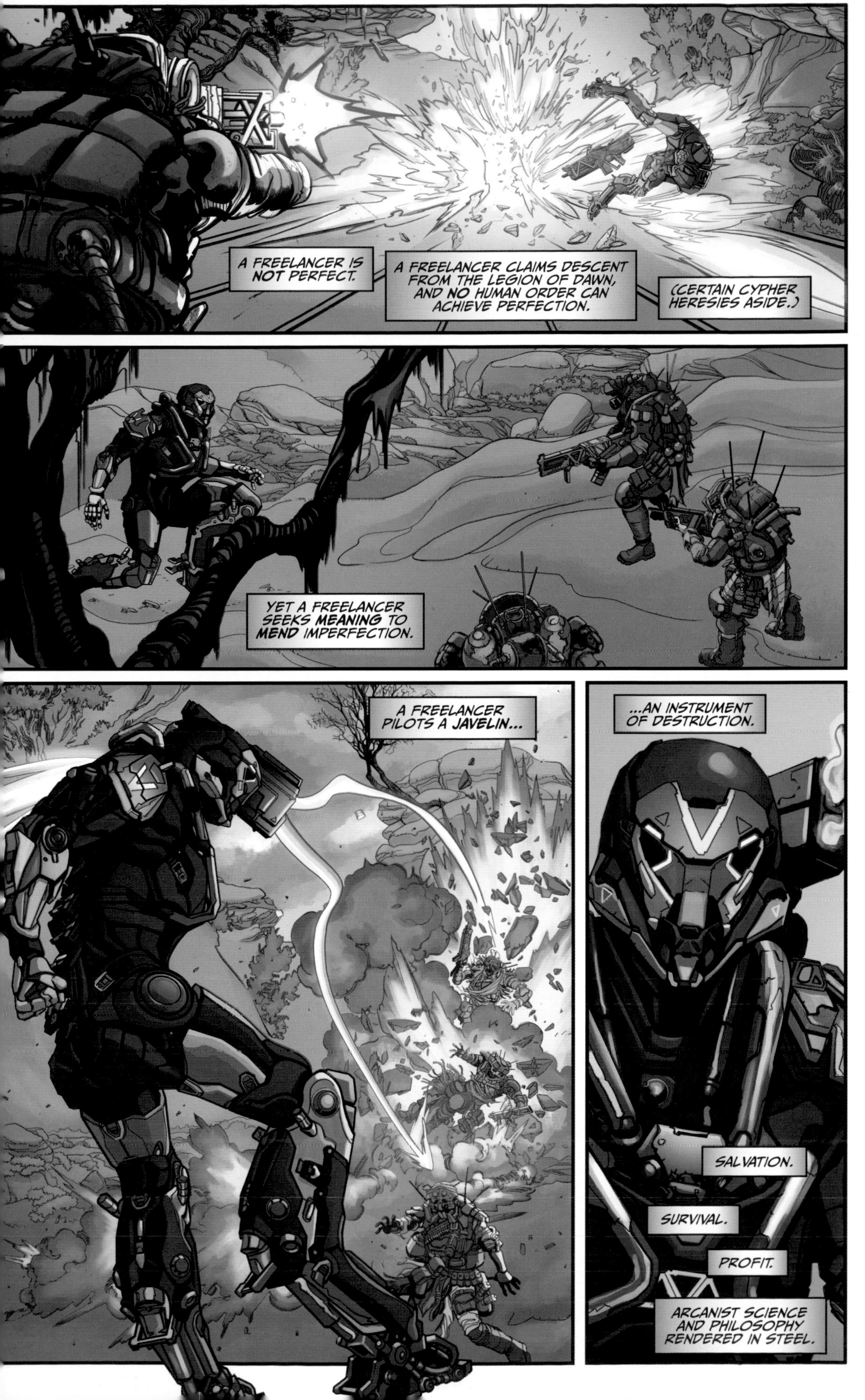
A FREELANCER IS NOT PERFECT.
A FREELANCER CLAIMS DESCENT FROM THE LEGION OF DAWN, AND NO HUMAN ORDER CAN ACHIEVE PERFECTION.
(CERTAIN CYPHER HERESIES ASIDE.)
YET A FREELANCER SEEKS MEANING TO MEND IMPERFECTION.
A FREELANCER PILOTS A JAVELIN...
...AN INSTRUMENT OF DESTRUCTION.
SALVATION.
SURVIVAL.
PROFIT.
ARCANIST SCIENCE AND PHILOSOPHY RENDERED IN STEEL.

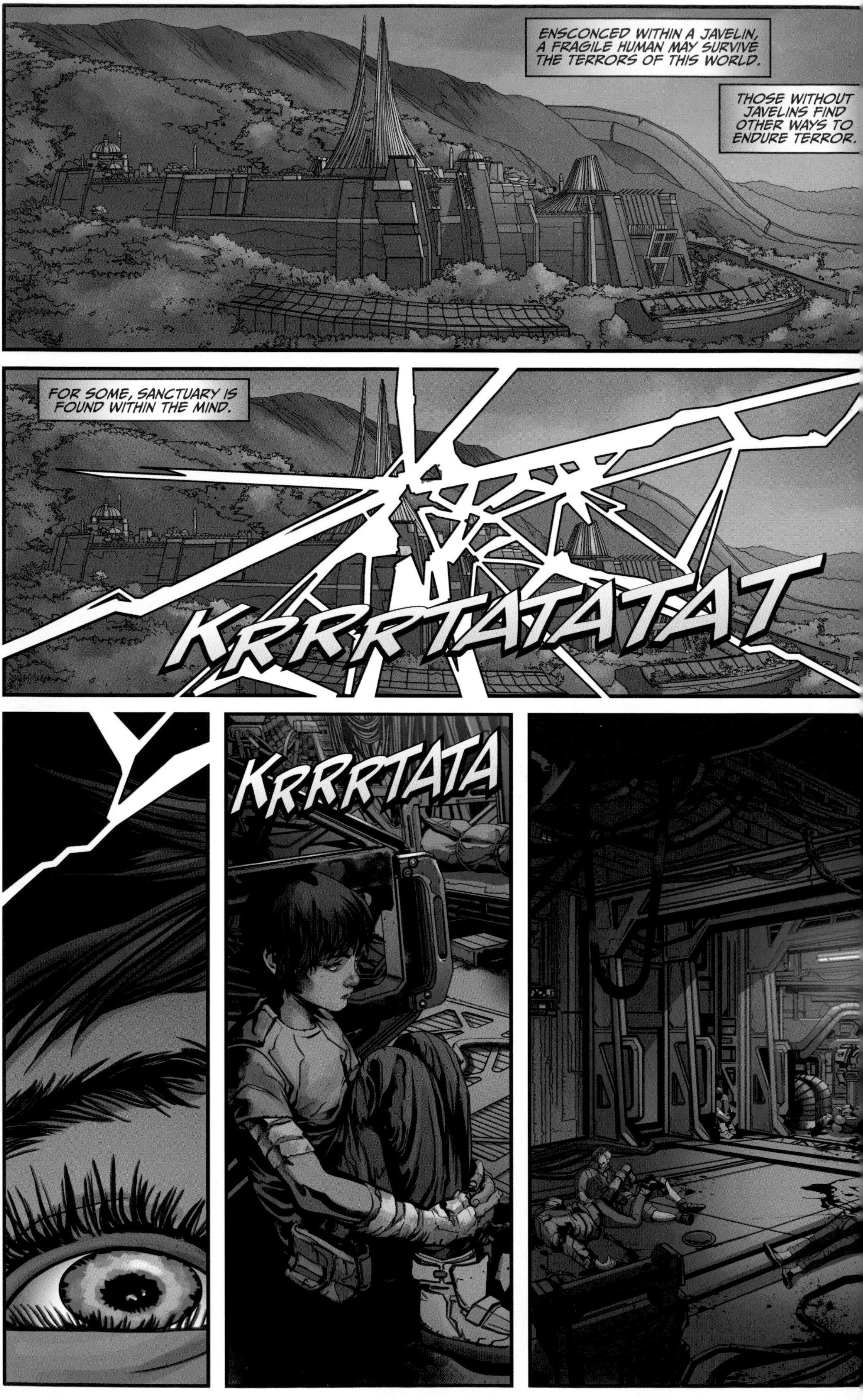
ENSCONCED WITHIN A JAVELIN, A FRAGILE HUMAN MAY SURVIVE THE TERRORS OF THIS WORLD.
THOSE WITHOUT JAVELINS FIND OTHER WAYS TO ENDURE TERROR.
FOR SOME, SANCTUARY IS FOUND WITHIN THE MIND.
KRRRTATATAT
KRRRTATA

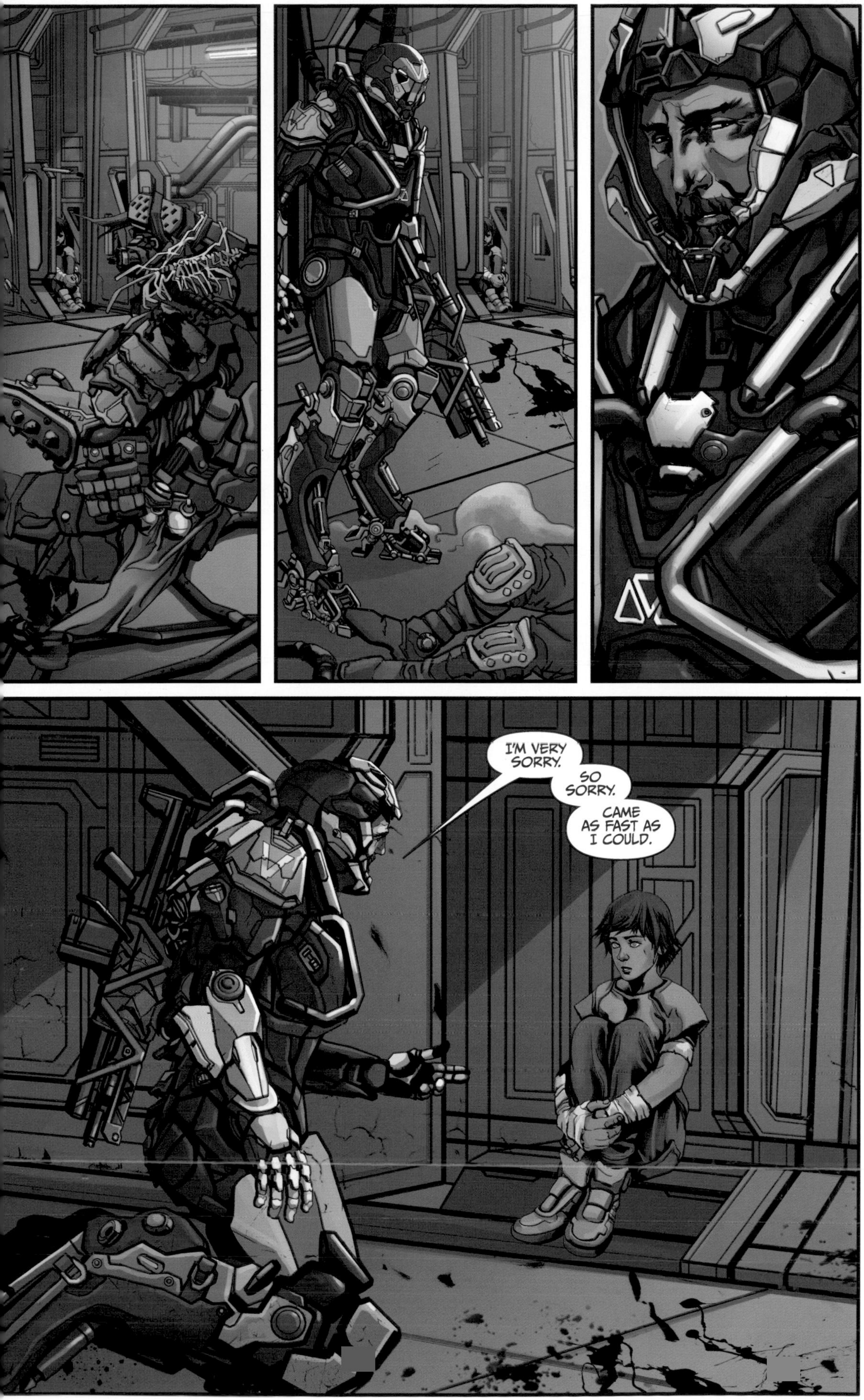
I'M VERY SORRY.
SO SORRY.
CAME AS FAST AS I COULD.

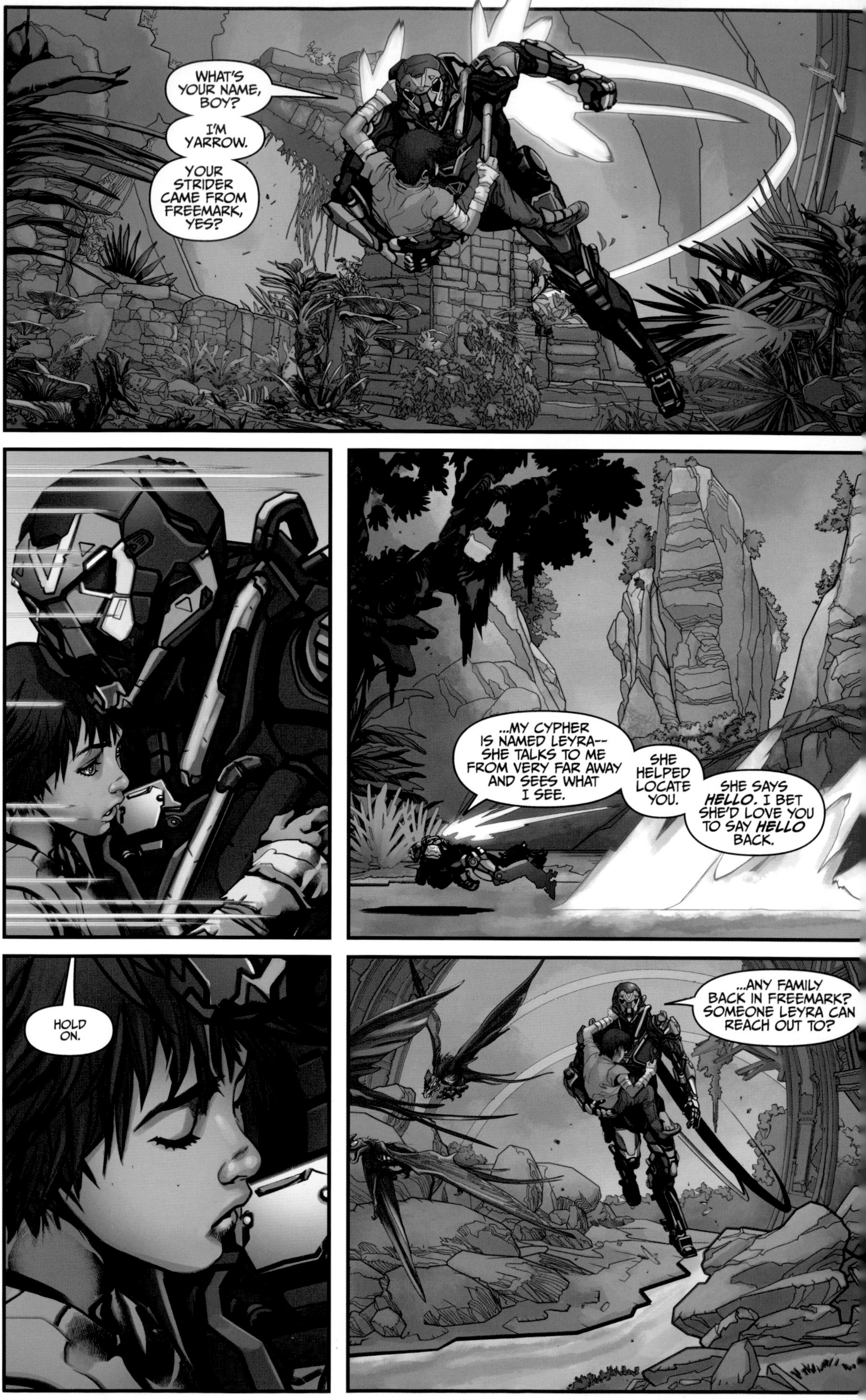
WHAT'S YOUR NAME, BOY?
I'M YARROW.
YOUR STRIDER CAME FROM FREEMARK, YES?
...MY CYPHER IS NAMED LEYRA-- SHE TALKS TO ME FROM VERY FAR AWAY AND SEES WHAT I SEE.
SHE HELPED LOCATE YOU.
SHE SAYS HELLO. I BET SHE'D LOVE YOU TO SAY HELLO BACK.
HOLD ON.
...ANY FAMILY BACK IN FREEMARK? SOMEONE LEYRA CAN REACH OUT TO?

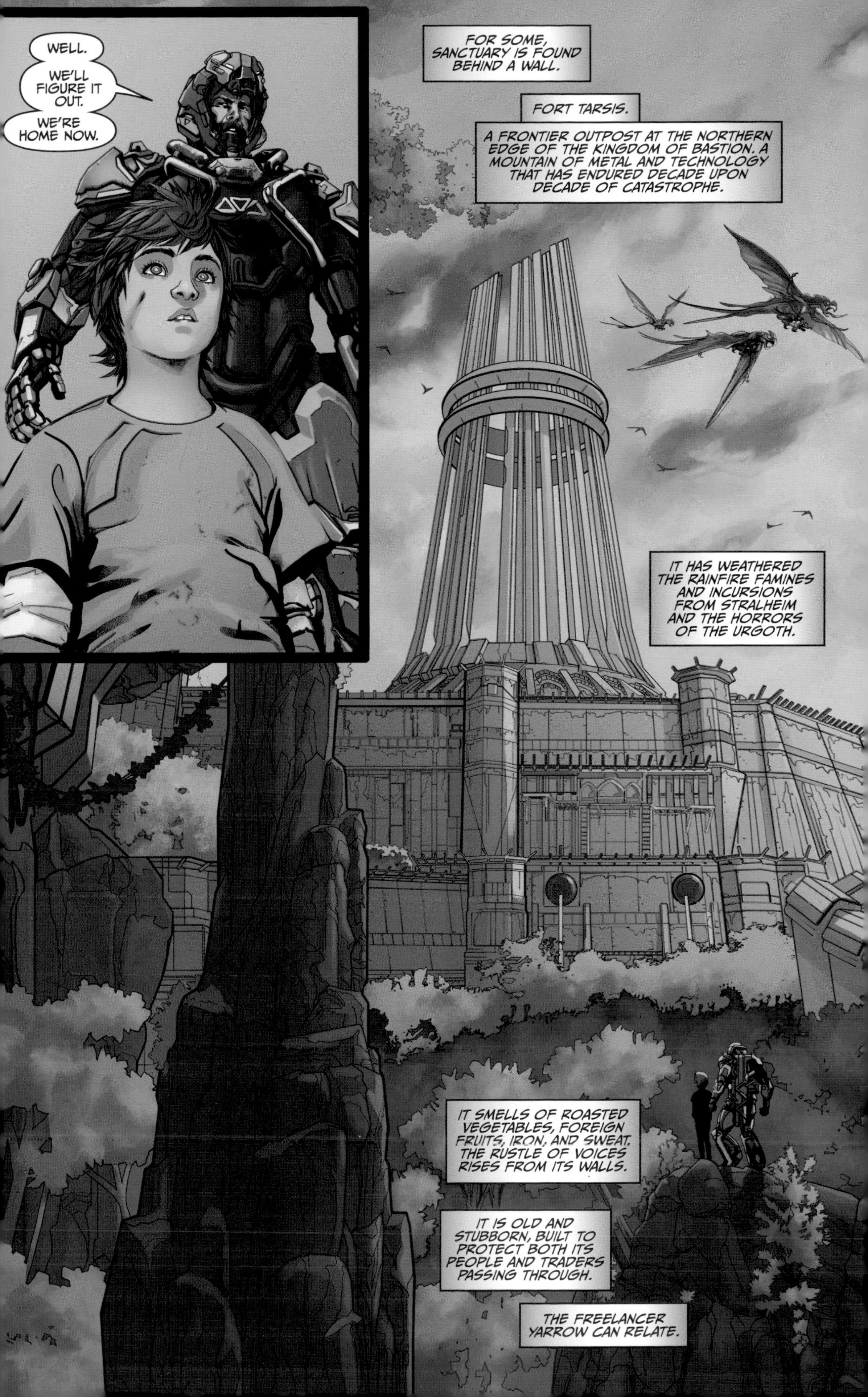
WELL.
WE'LL FIGURE IT OUT.
WE'RE HOME NOW.
FOR SOME, SANCTUARY IS FOUND BEHIND A WALL.
FORT TARSIS.
A FRONTIER OUTPOST AT THE NORTHERN EDGE OF THE KINGDOM OF BASTION. A MOUNTAIN OF METAL AND TECHNOLOGY THAT HAS ENDURED DECADE UPON DECADE OF CATASTROPHE.
IT HAS WEATHERED THE RAINFIRE FAMINES AND INCURSIONS FROM STRALHEIM AND THE HORRORS OF THE URGOTH.
IT SMELLS OF ROASTED VEGETABLES, FOREIGN FRUITS, IRON, AND SWEAT. THE RUSTLE OF VOICES RISES FROM ITS WALLS.
IT IS OLD AND STUBBORN, BUILT TO PROTECT BOTH ITS PEOPLE AND TRADERS PASSING THROUGH.
THE FREELANCER YARROW CAN RELATE.

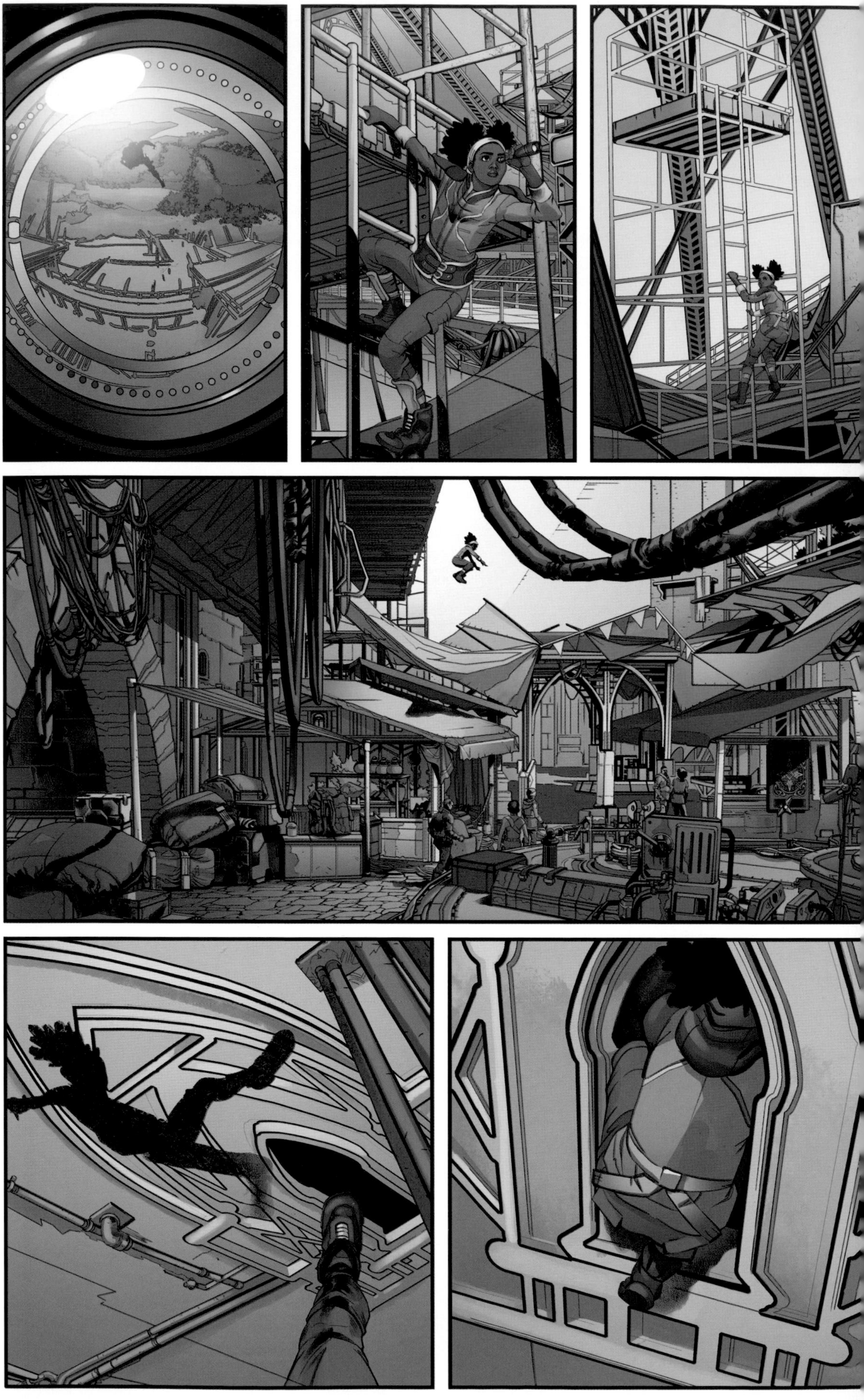

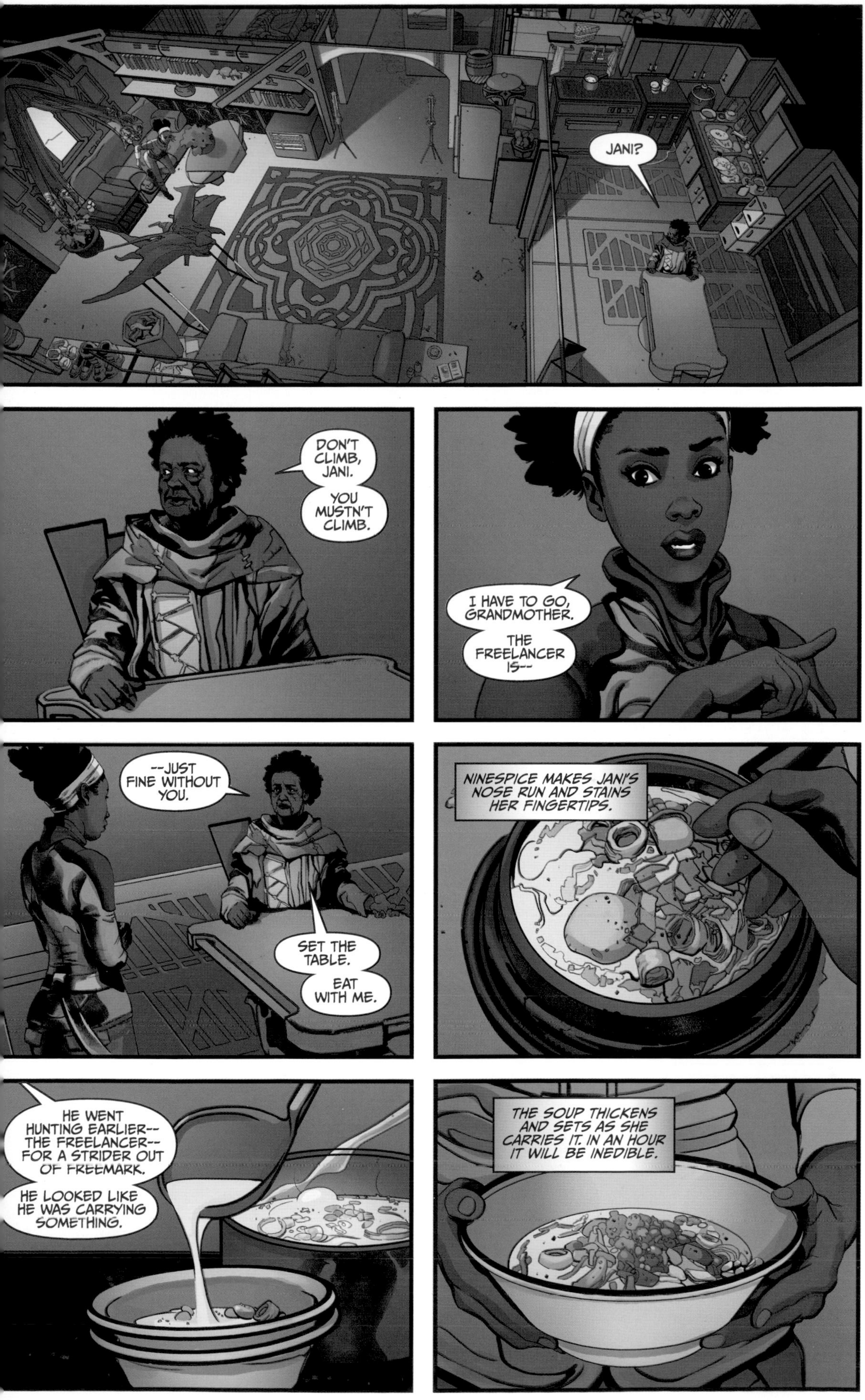
JANI?
DON'T CLIMB, JANI.
YOU MUSTN'T CLIMB.
I HAVE TO GO, GRANDMOTHER.
THE FREELANCER IS--
--JUST FINE WITHOUT YOU.
SET THE TABLE.
EAT WITH ME.
NINESPICE MAKES JANI'S NOSE RUN AND STAINS HER FINGERTIPS.
HE WENT HUNTING EARLIER-- THE FREELANCER-- FOR A STRIDER OUT OF FREEMARK.
HE LOOKED LIKE HE WAS CARRYING SOMETHING.
THE SOUP THICKENS AND SETS AS SHE CARRIES IT. IN AN HOUR IT WILL BE INEDIBLE.

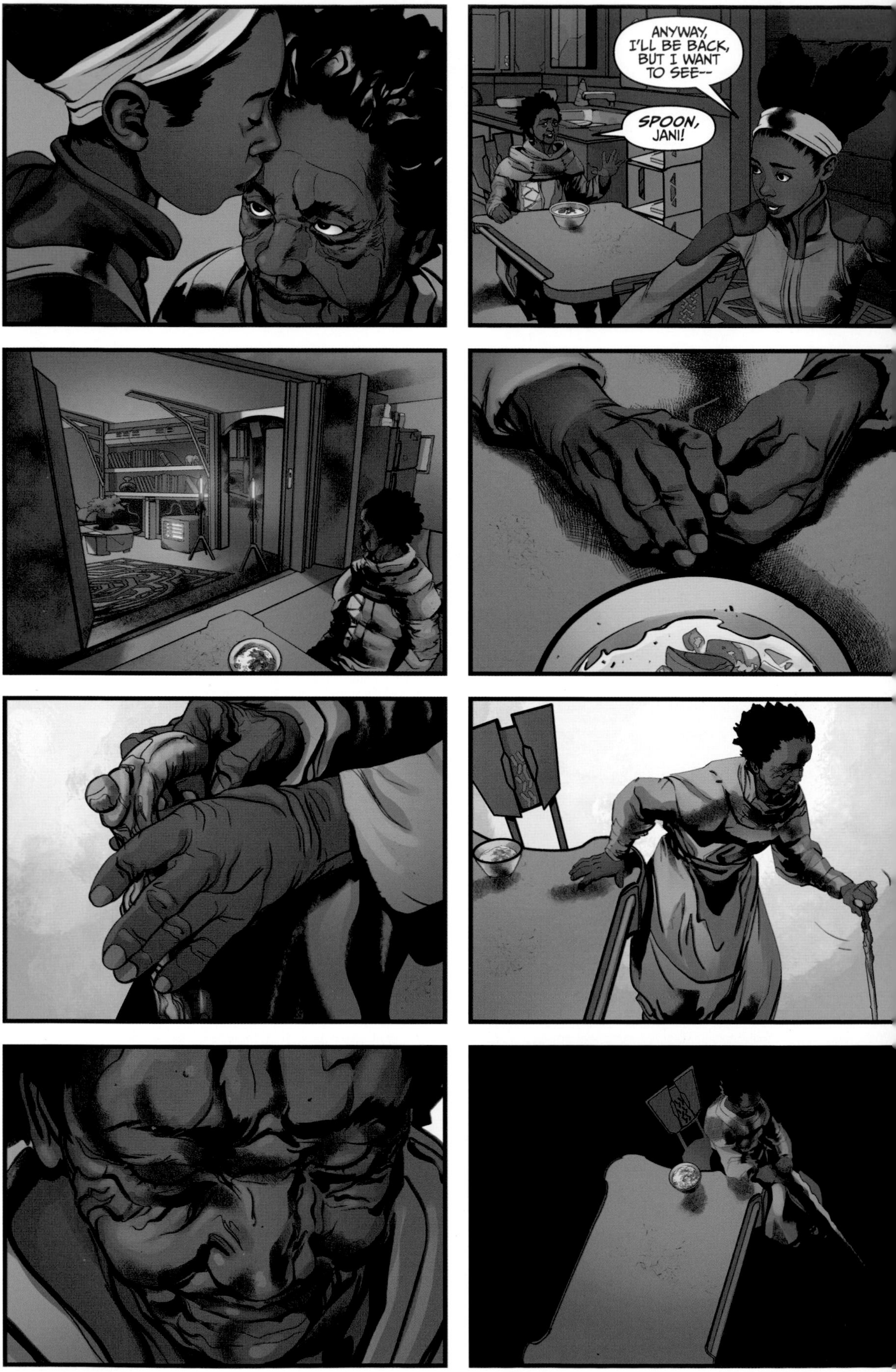
ANYWAY, I'LL BE BACK, BUT I WANT TO SEE--
SPOON, JANI!

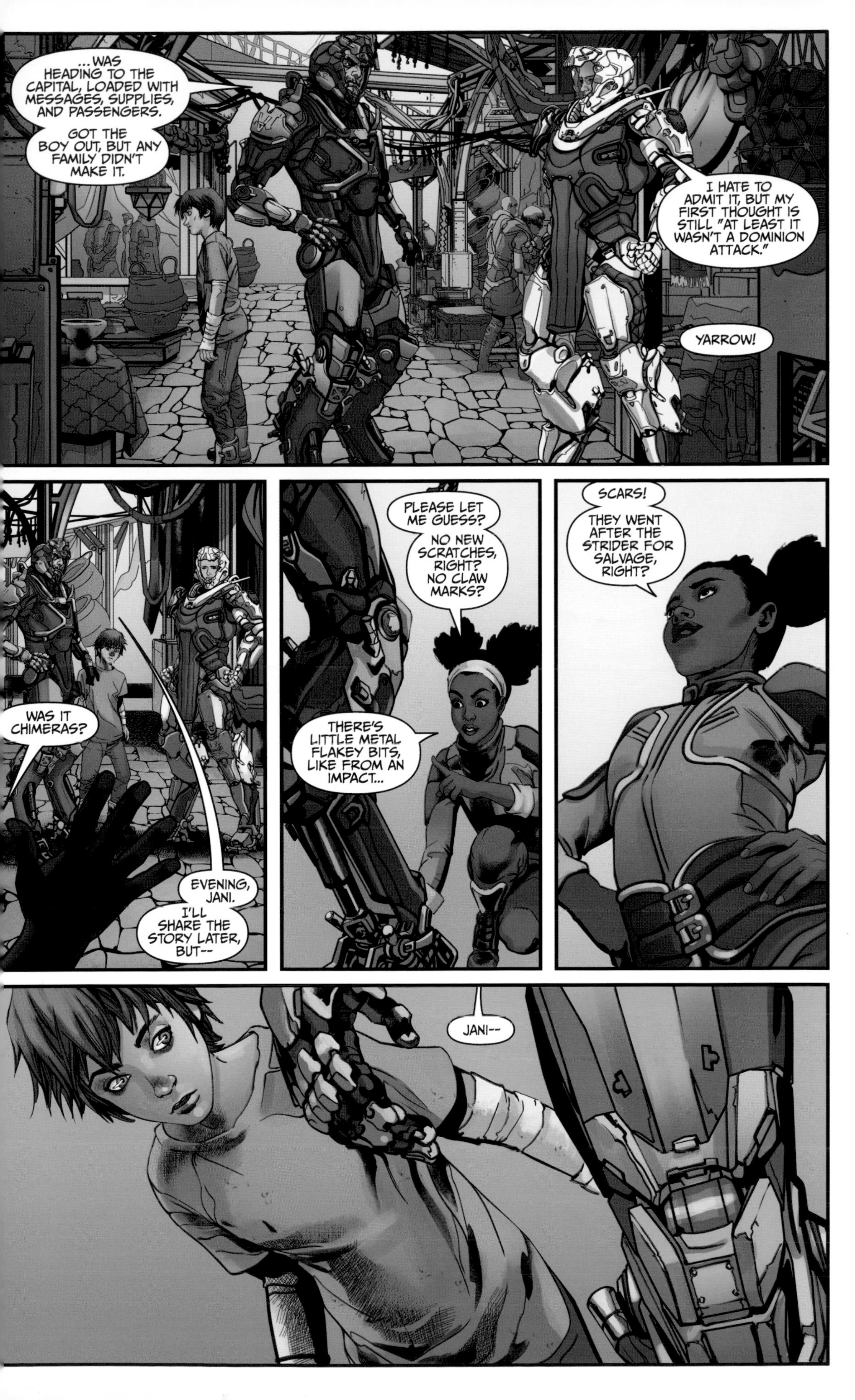
...WAS HEADING TO THE CAPITAL, LOADED WITH MESSAGES, SUPPLIES, AND PASSENGERS.
GOT THE BOY OUT, BUT ANY FAMILY DIDN'T MAKE IT.
I HATE TO ADMIT IT, BUT MY FIRST THOUGHT IS STILL "AT LEAST IT WASN'T A DOMINION ATTACK."
YARROW!
WAS IT CHIMERAS?
EVENING, JANI.
I'LL SHARE THE STORY LATER, BUT--
PLEASE LET ME GUESS?
NO NEW SCRATCHES, RIGHT? NO CLAW MARKS?
THERE'S LITTLE METAL FLAKEY BITS, LIKE FROM AN IMPACT...
SCARS!
THEY WENT AFTER THE STRIDER FOR SALVAGE, RIGHT?
JANI--

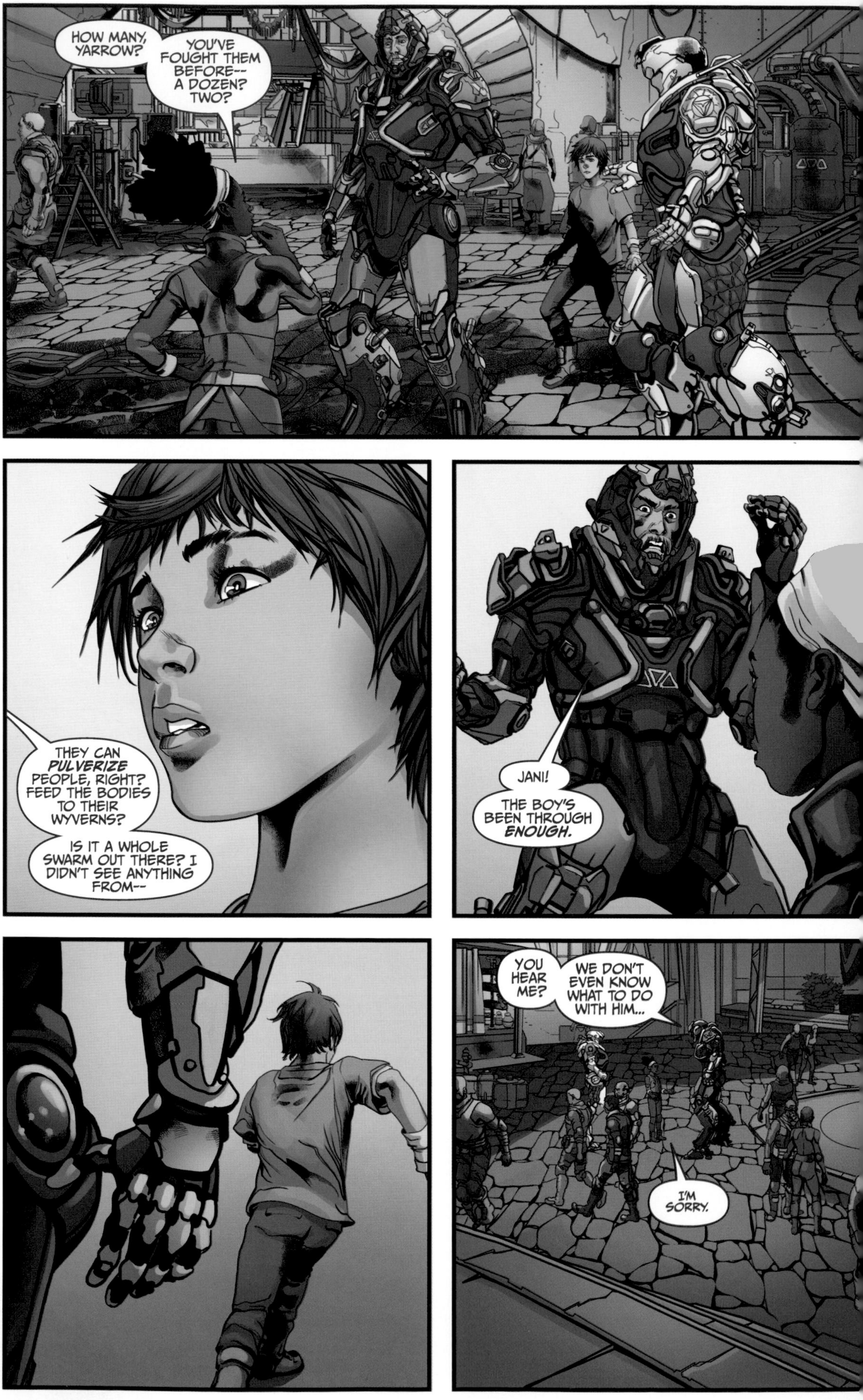
HOW MANY, YARROW?
YOU'VE FOUGHT THEM BEFORE-- A DOZEN? TWO?
THEY CAN *PULVERIZE* PEOPLE, RIGHT? FEED THE BODIES TO THEIR WYVERNS?
IS IT A WHOLE SWARM OUT THERE? I DIDN'T SEE ANYTHING FROM--
JANI!
THE BOY'S BEEN THROUGH *ENOUGH.*
YOU HEAR ME?
WE DON'T EVEN KNOW WHAT TO DO WITH HIM...
I'M SORRY.

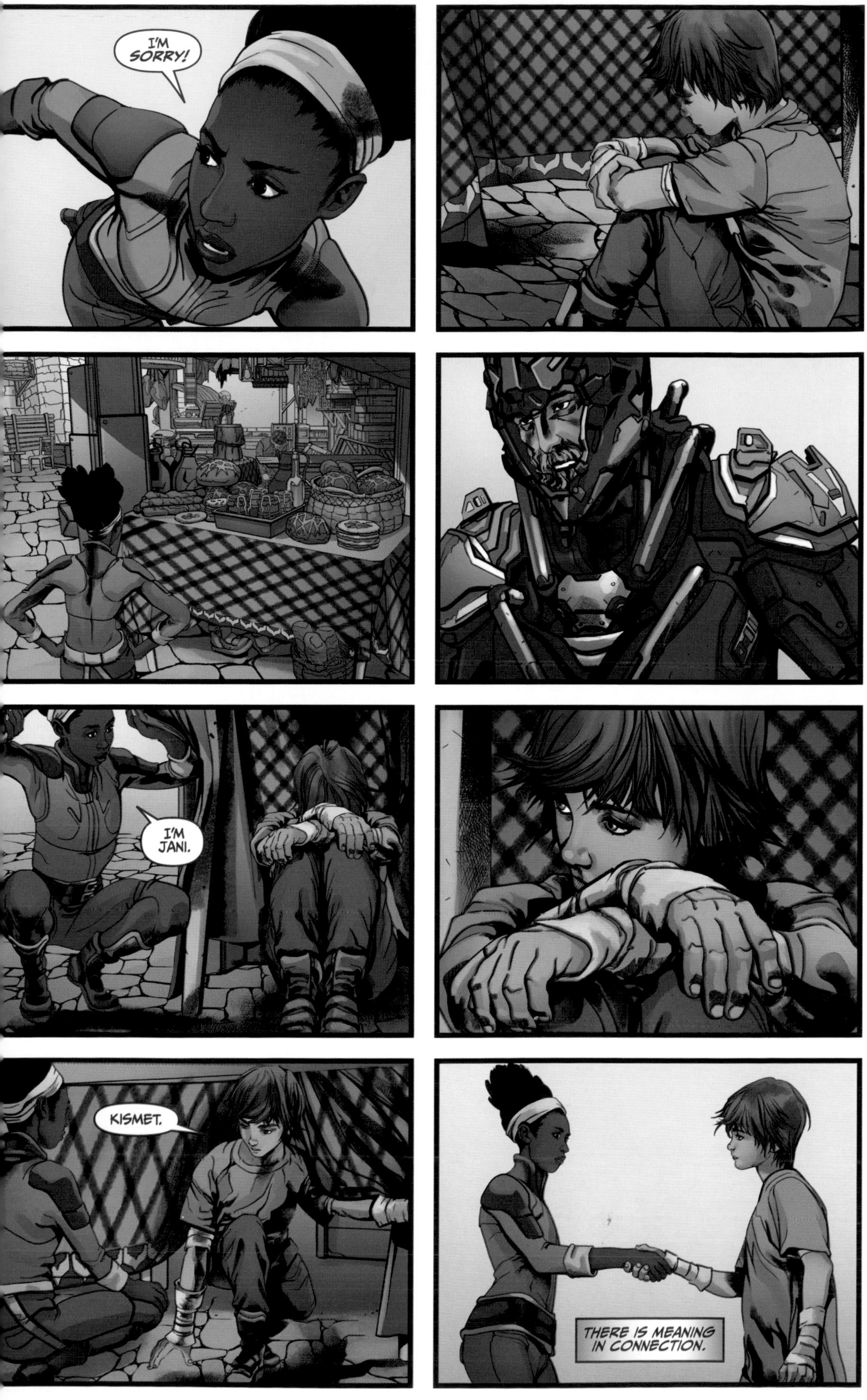
I'M SORRY!
I'M JANI.
KISMET.
THERE IS MEANING IN CONNECTION.

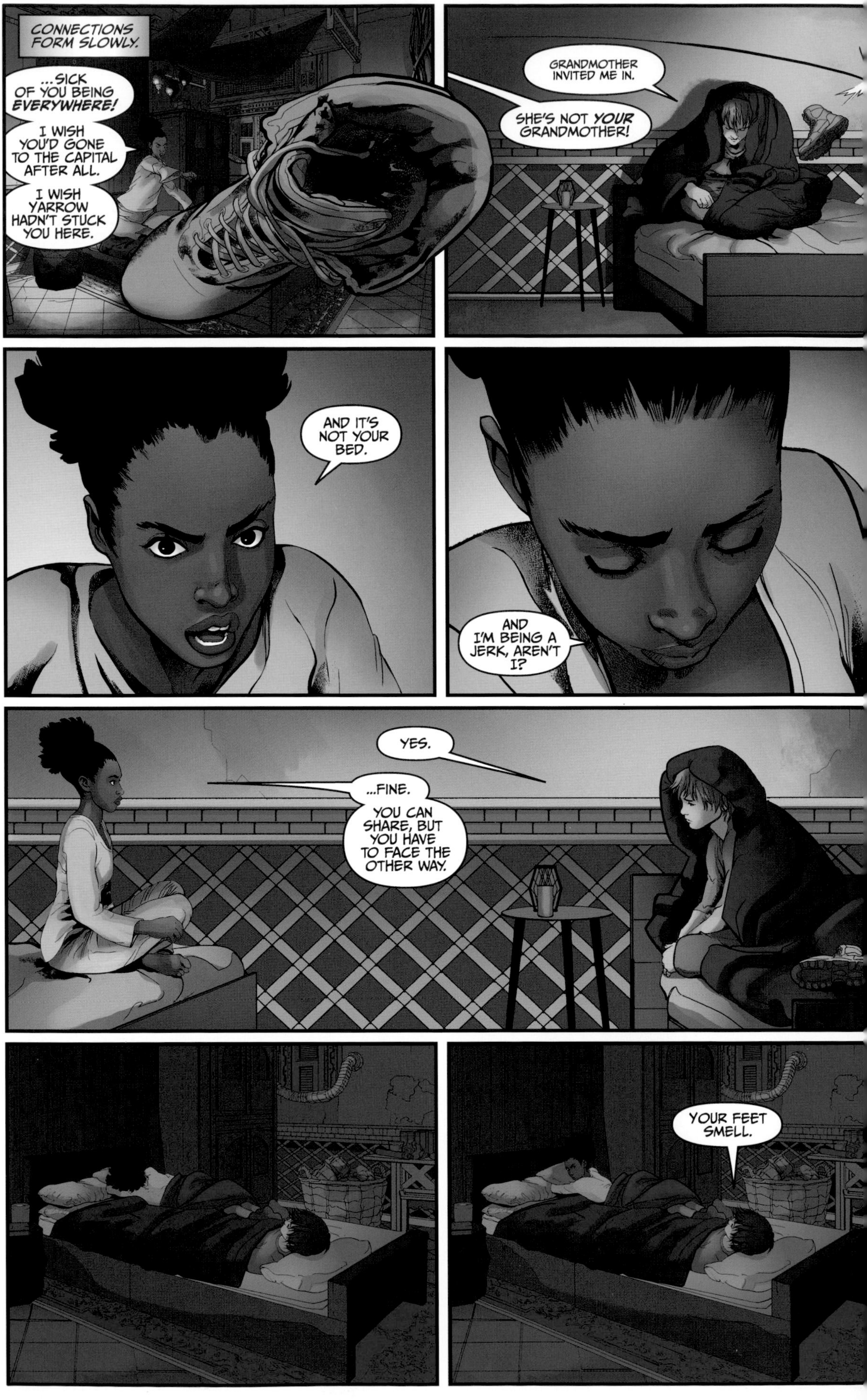
CONNECTIONS FORM SLOWLY.
...SICK OF YOU BEING EVERYWHERE!
I WISH YOU'D GONE TO THE CAPITAL AFTER ALL.
I WISH YARROW HADN'T STUCK YOU HERE.
GRANDMOTHER INVITED ME IN.
SHE'S NOT YOUR GRANDMOTHER!
AND IT'S NOT YOUR BED.
AND I'M BEING A JERK, AREN'T I?
YES.
...FINE.
YOU CAN SHARE, BUT YOU HAVE TO FACE THE OTHER WAY.
YOUR FEET SMELL.

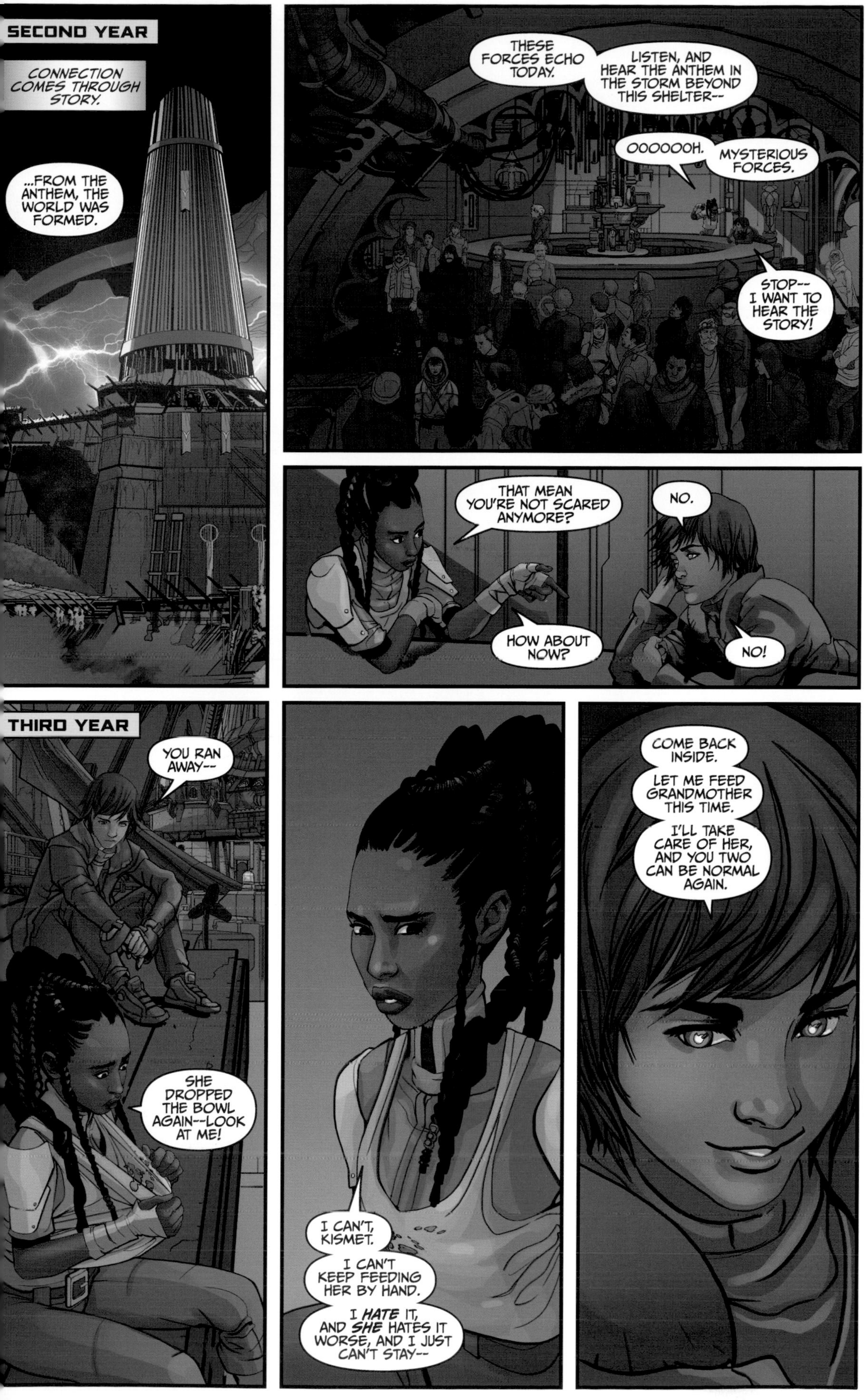
SECOND YEAR
CONNECTION COMES THROUGH STORY.
...FROM THE ANTHEM, THE WORLD WAS FORMED.
THESE FORCES ECHO TODAY.
LISTEN, AND HEAR THE ANTHEM IN THE STORM BEYOND THIS SHELTER--
OOOOOOH.
MYSTERIOUS FORCES.
STOP-- I WANT TO HEAR THE STORY!
THAT MEAN YOU'RE NOT SCARED ANYMORE?
NO.
HOW ABOUT NOW?
NO!
THIRD YEAR
YOU RAN AWAY--
SHE DROPPED THE BOWL AGAIN--LOOK AT ME!
I CAN'T, KISMET.
I CAN'T KEEP FEEDING HER BY HAND.
I *HATE* IT, AND *SHE* HATES IT WORSE, AND I JUST CAN'T STAY--
COME BACK INSIDE.
LET ME FEED GRANDMOTHER THIS TIME.
I'LL TAKE CARE OF HER, AND YOU TWO CAN BE NORMAL AGAIN.

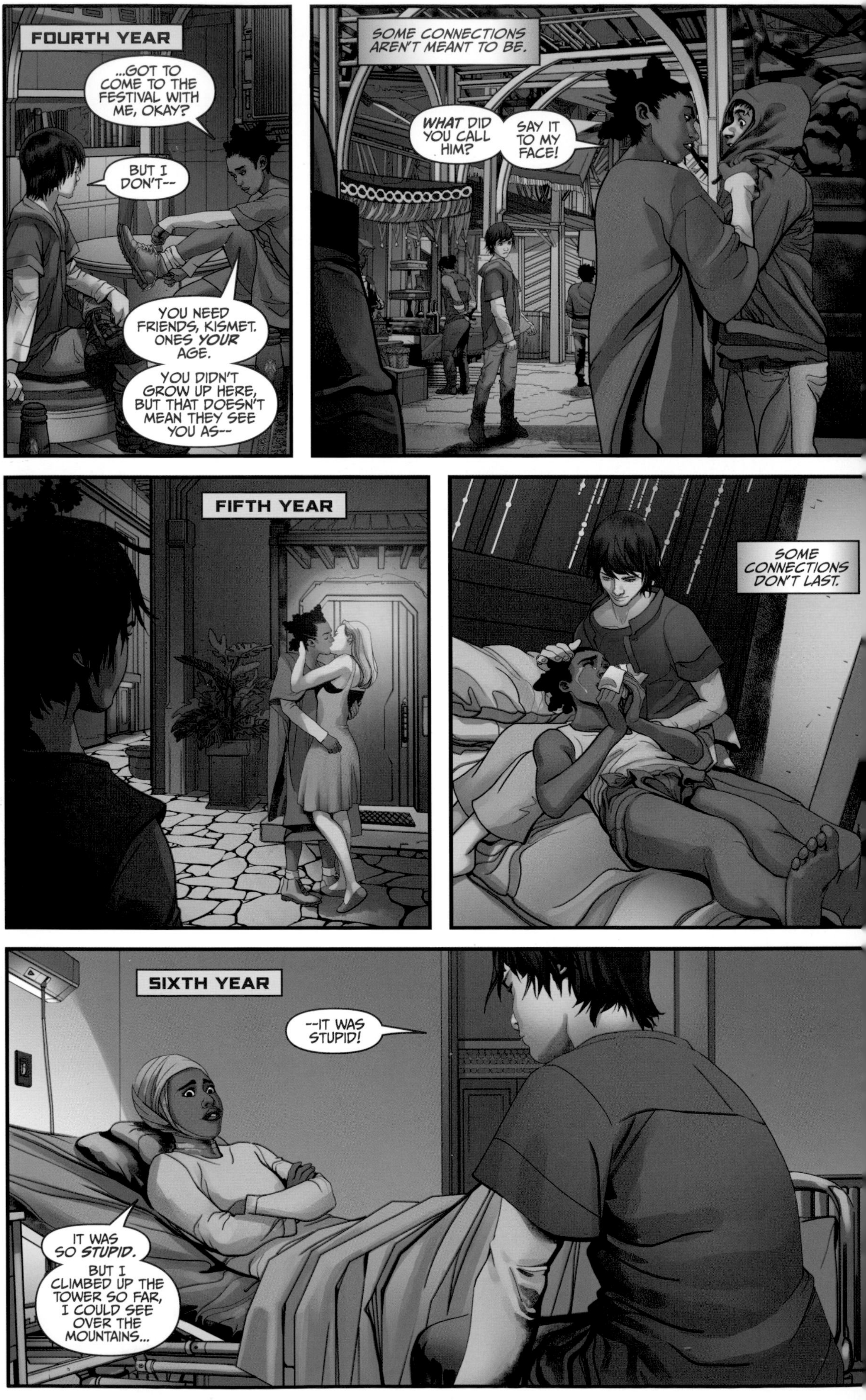
FOURTH YEAR
...GOT TO COME TO THE FESTIVAL WITH ME, OKAY?
BUT I DON'T--
YOU NEED FRIENDS, KISMET. ONES YOUR AGE.
YOU DIDN'T GROW UP HERE, BUT THAT DOESN'T MEAN THEY SEE YOU AS--
SOME CONNECTIONS AREN'T MEANT TO BE.
WHAT DID YOU CALL HIM?
SAY IT TO MY FACE!
FIFTH YEAR
SOME CONNECTIONS DON'T LAST.
SIXTH YEAR
--IT WAS STUPID!
IT WAS SO STUPID.
BUT I CLIMBED UP THE TOWER SO FAR, I COULD SEE OVER THE MOUNTAINS...

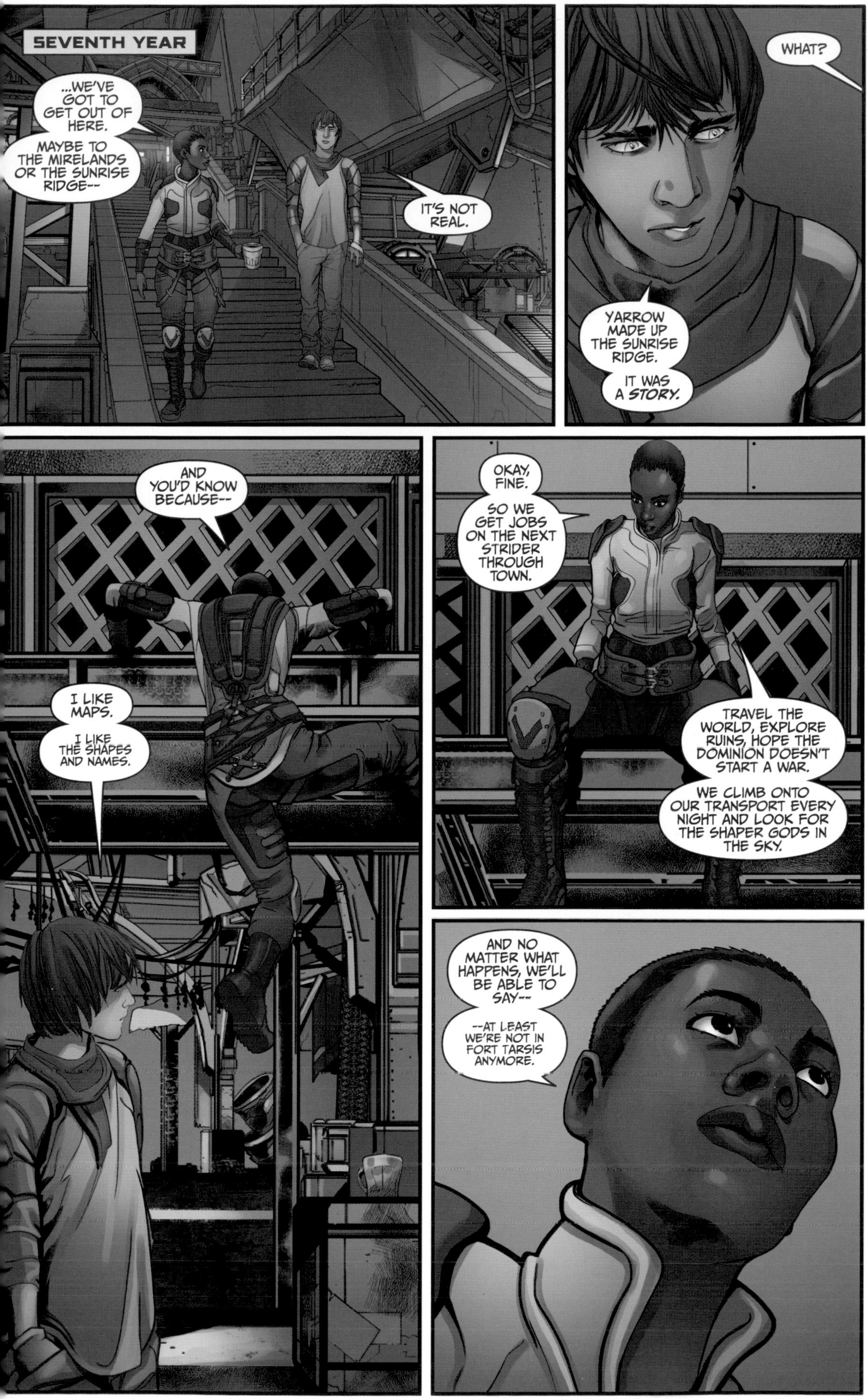
SEVENTH YEAR
...WE'VE GOT TO GET OUT OF HERE.
MAYBE TO THE MIRELANDS OR THE SUNRISE RIDGE--
IT'S NOT REAL.
WHAT?
YARROW MADE UP THE SUNRISE RIDGE.
IT WAS A *STORY.*
AND YOU'D KNOW BECAUSE--
I LIKE MAPS.
I LIKE THE SHAPES AND NAMES.
OKAY, FINE.
SO WE GET JOBS ON THE NEXT STRIDER THROUGH TOWN.
TRAVEL THE WORLD, EXPLORE RUINS, HOPE THE DOMINION DOESN'T START A WAR.
WE CLIMB ONTO OUR TRANSPORT EVERY NIGHT AND LOOK FOR THE SHAPER GODS IN THE SKY.
AND NO MATTER WHAT HAPPENS, WE'LL BE ABLE TO SAY--
--AT LEAST WE'RE NOT IN FORT TARSIS ANYMORE.

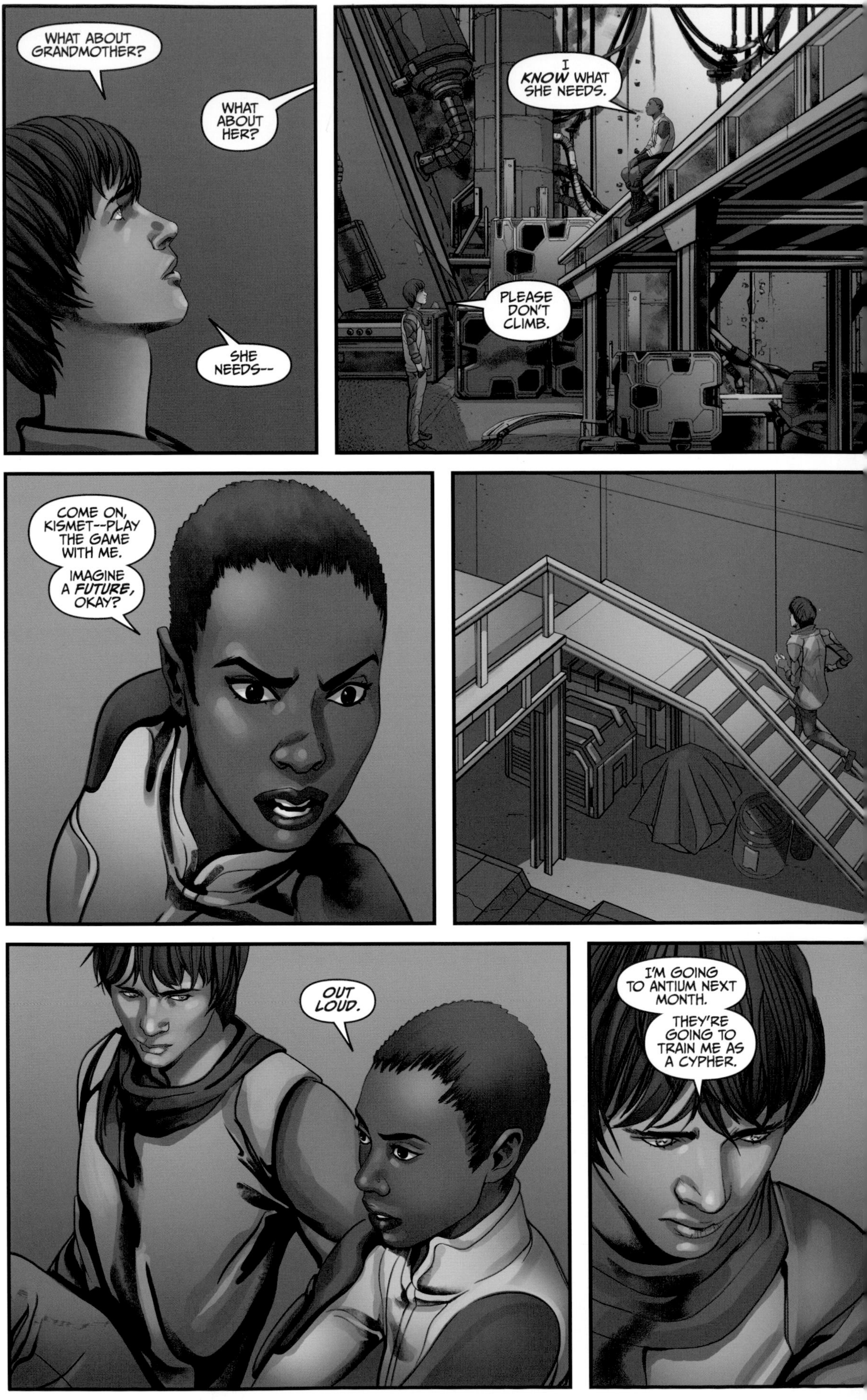
WHAT ABOUT GRANDMOTHER?
WHAT ABOUT HER?
SHE NEEDS--
I KNOW WHAT SHE NEEDS.
PLEASE DON'T CLIMB.
COME ON, KISMET--PLAY THE GAME WITH ME.
IMAGINE A FUTURE, OKAY?
OUT LOUD.
I'M GOING TO ANTIUM NEXT MONTH.
THEY'RE GOING TO TRAIN ME AS A CYPHER.

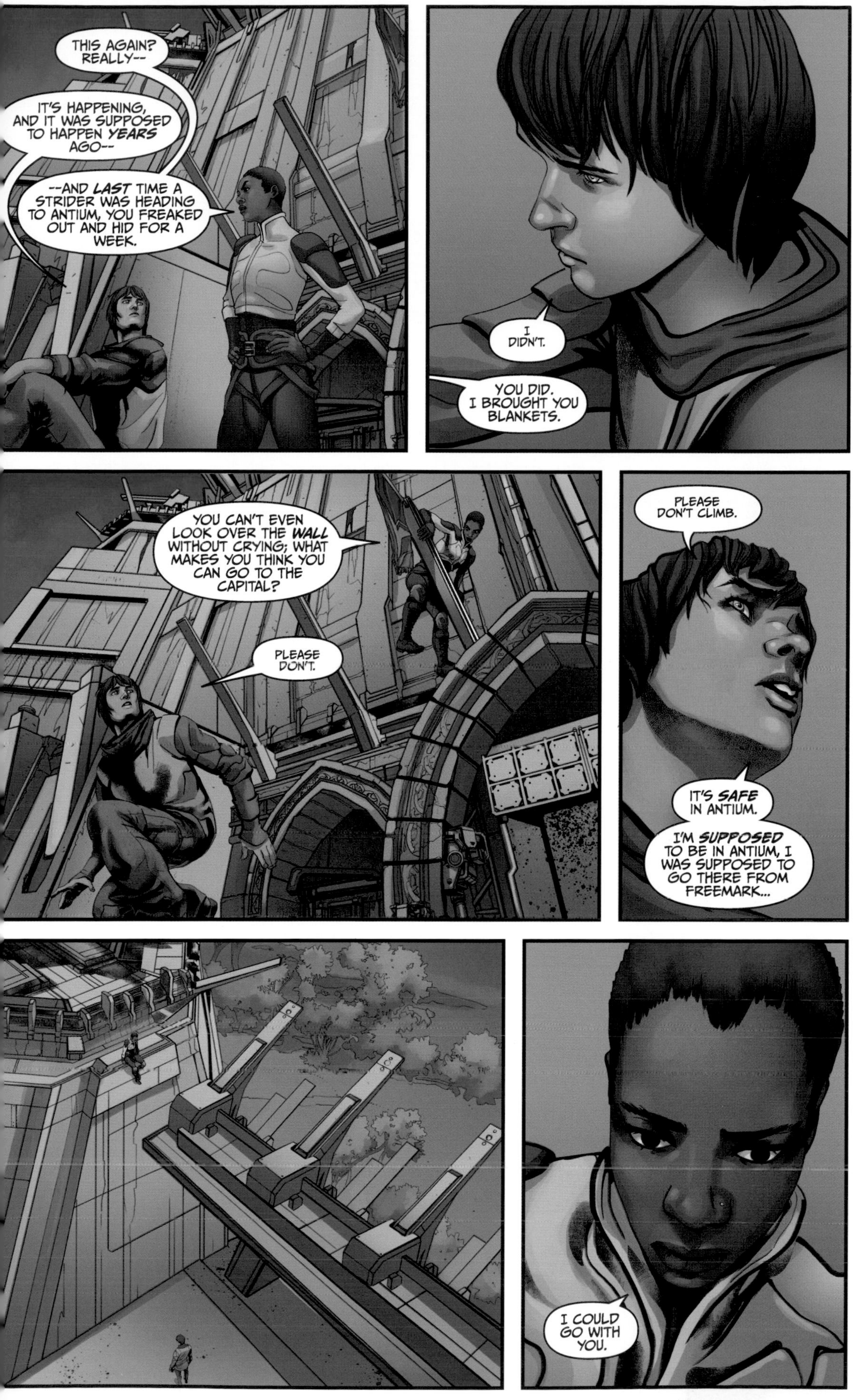
THIS AGAIN? REALLY--
IT'S HAPPENING, AND IT WAS SUPPOSED TO HAPPEN YEARS AGO--
--AND LAST TIME A STRIDER WAS HEADING TO ANTIUM, YOU FREAKED OUT AND HID FOR A WEEK.
I DIDN'T.
YOU DID. I BROUGHT YOU BLANKETS.
YOU CAN'T EVEN LOOK OVER THE WALL WITHOUT CRYING; WHAT MAKES YOU THINK YOU CAN GO TO THE CAPITAL?
PLEASE DON'T.
PLEASE DON'T CLIMB.
IT'S SAFE IN ANTIUM.
I'M SUPPOSED TO BE IN ANTIUM, I WAS SUPPOSED TO GO THERE FROM FREEMARK...
I COULD GO WITH YOU.

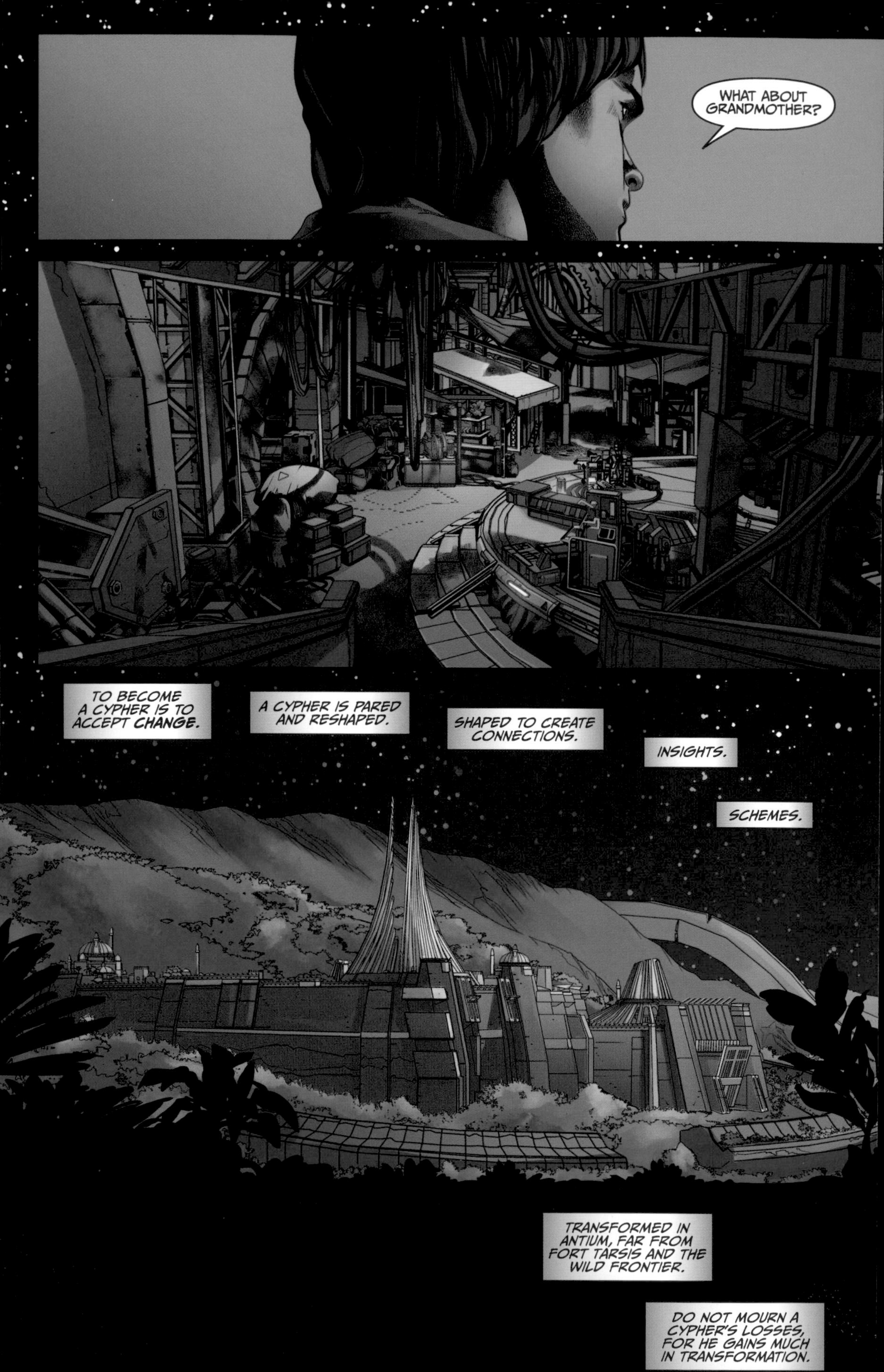
WHAT ABOUT GRANDMOTHER?
TO BECOME A CYPHER IS TO ACCEPT CHANGE.
A CYPHER IS PARED AND RESHAPED.
SHAPED TO CREATE CONNECTIONS.
INSIGHTS.
SCHEMES.
TRANSFORMED IN ANTIUM, FAR FROM FORT TARSIS AND THE WILD FRONTIER.
DO NOT MOURN A CYPHER'S LOSSES, FOR HE GAINS MUCH IN TRANSFORMATION.

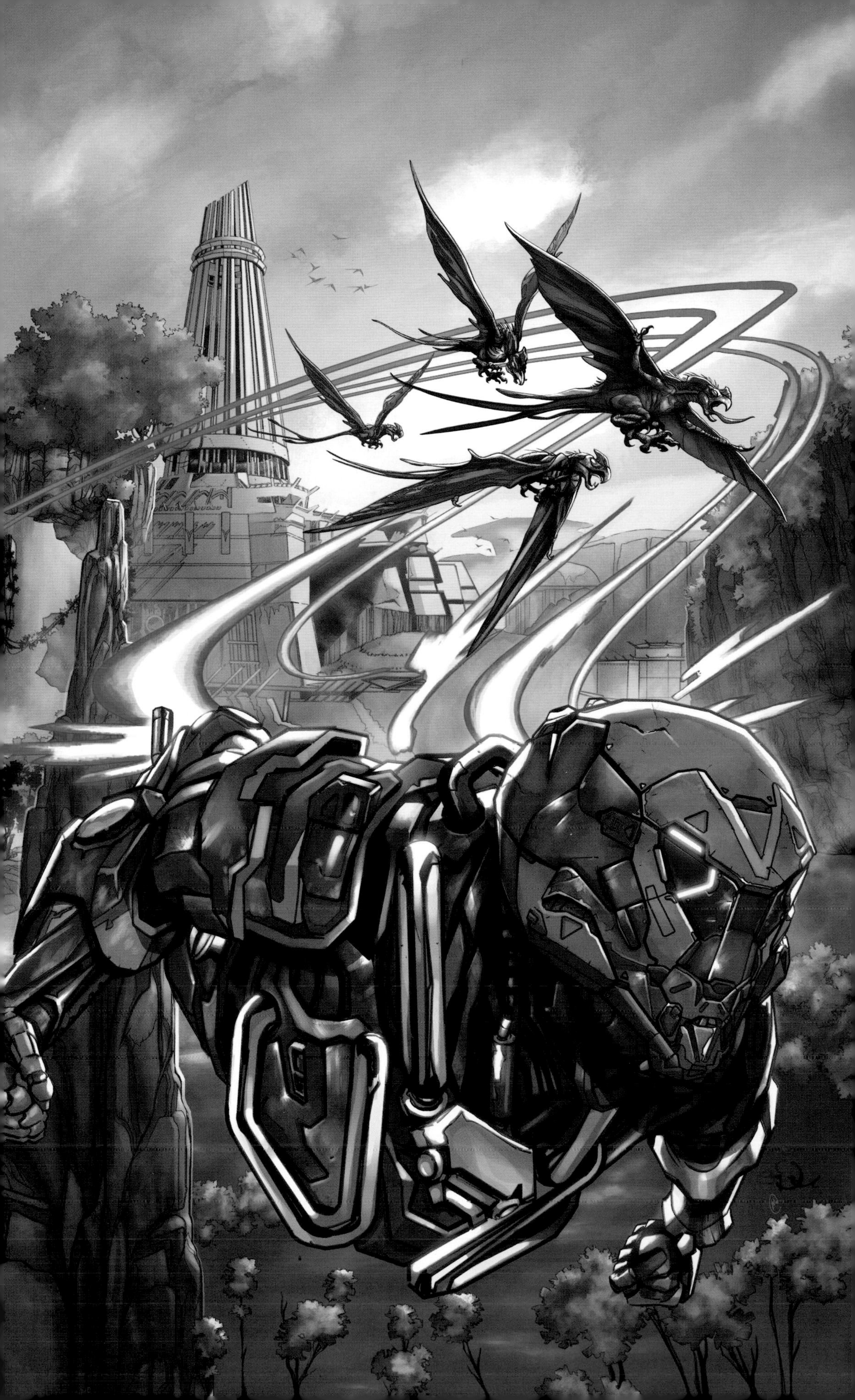

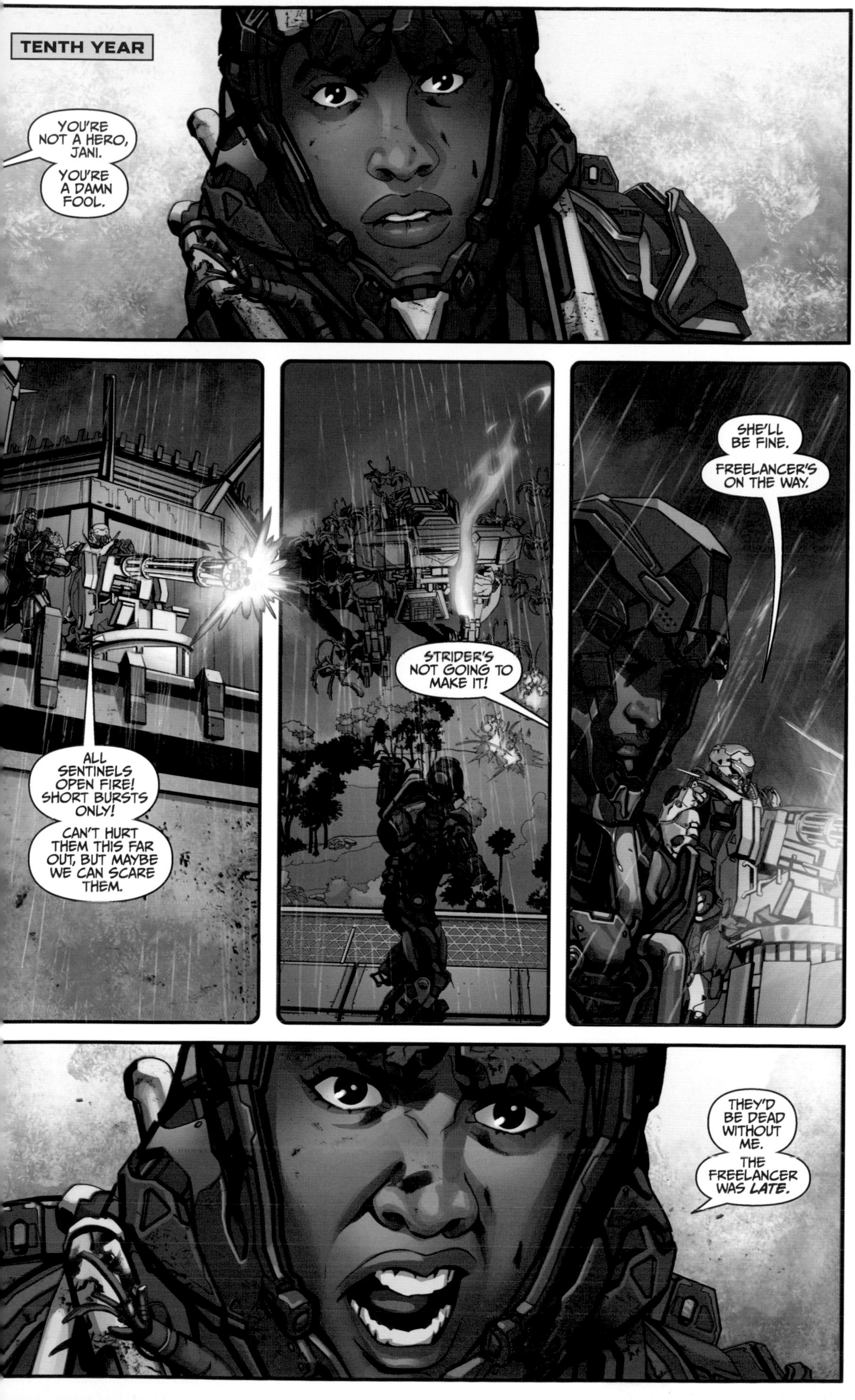
TENTH YEAR
YOU'RE NOT A HERO, JANI.
YOU'RE A DAMN FOOL.
ALL SENTINELS OPEN FIRE! SHORT BURSTS ONLY!
CAN'T HURT THEM THIS FAR OUT, BUT MAYBE WE CAN SCARE THEM.
STRIDER'S NOT GOING TO MAKE IT!
SHE'LL BE FINE.
FREELANCER'S ON THE WAY.
THEY'D BE DEAD WITHOUT ME.
THE FREELANCER WAS *LATE.*

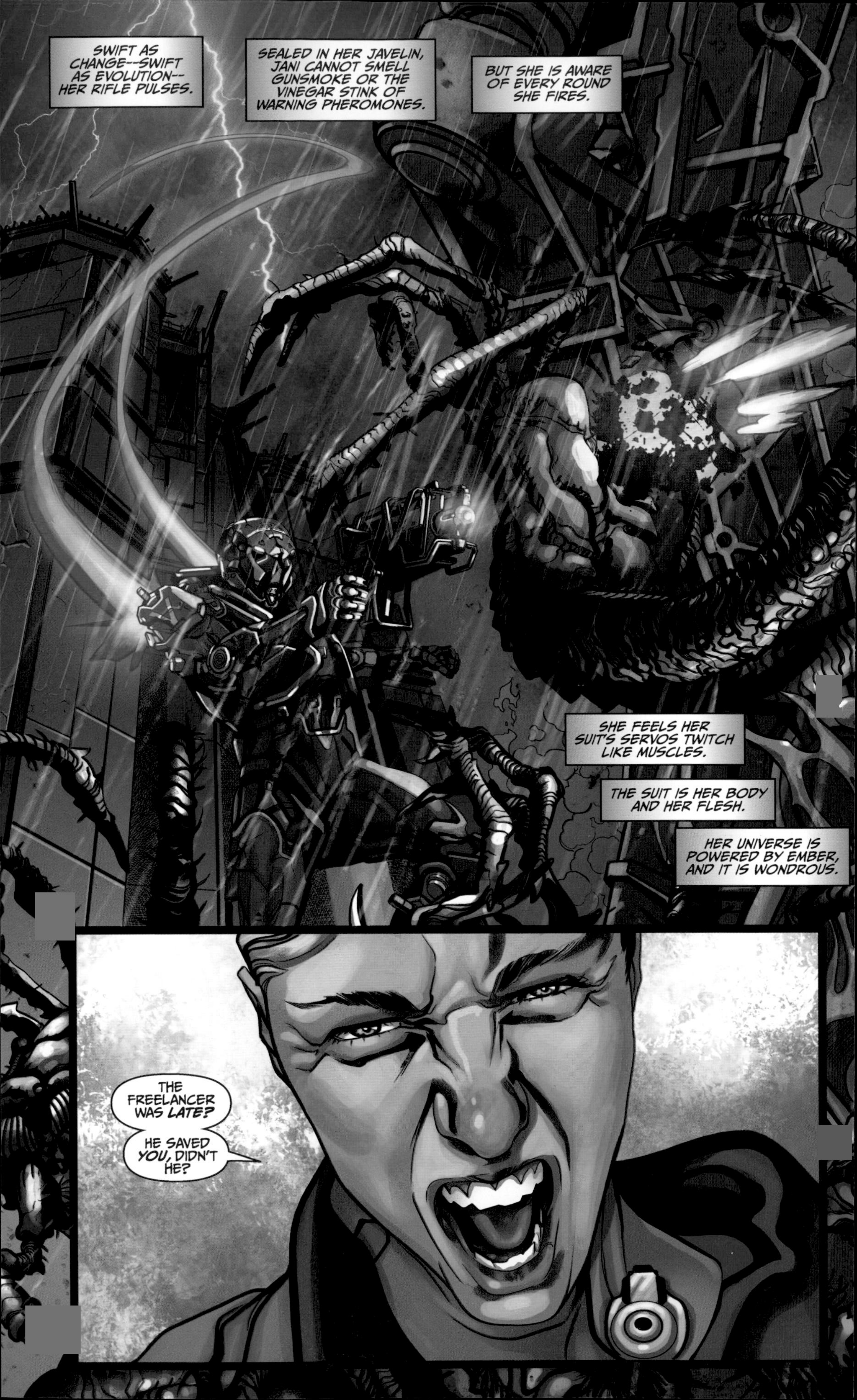
SWIFT AS CHANGE--SWIFT AS EVOLUTION--HER RIFLE PULSES.
SEALED IN HER JAVELIN, JANI CANNOT SMELL GUNSMOKE OR THE VINEGAR STINK OF WARNING PHEROMONES.
BUT SHE IS AWARE OF EVERY ROUND SHE FIRES.
SHE FEELS HER SUIT'S SERVOS TWITCH LIKE MUSCLES.
THE SUIT IS HER BODY AND HER FLESH.
HER UNIVERSE IS POWERED BY EMBER, AND IT IS WONDROUS.
THE FREELANCER WAS *LATE?*
HE SAVED *YOU*, DIDN'T HE?

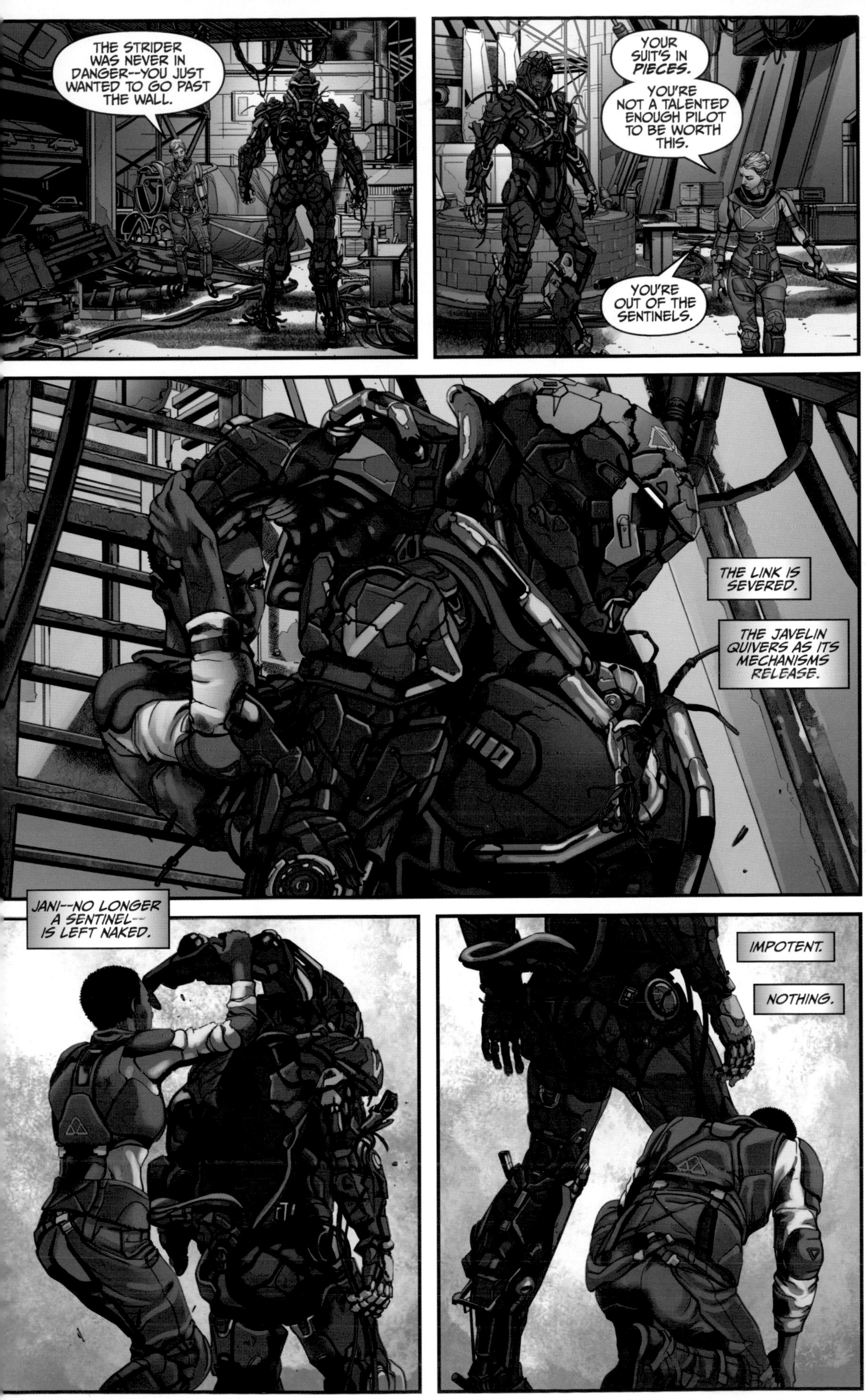
THE STRIDER WAS NEVER IN DANGER--YOU JUST WANTED TO GO PAST THE WALL.
YOUR SUIT'S IN PIECES.
YOU'RE NOT A TALENTED ENOUGH PILOT TO BE WORTH THIS.
YOU'RE OUT OF THE SENTINELS.
THE LINK IS SEVERED.
THE JAVELIN QUIVERS AS ITS MECHANISMS RELEASE.
JANI--NO LONGER A SENTINEL--IS LEFT NAKED.
IMPOTENT.
NOTHING.

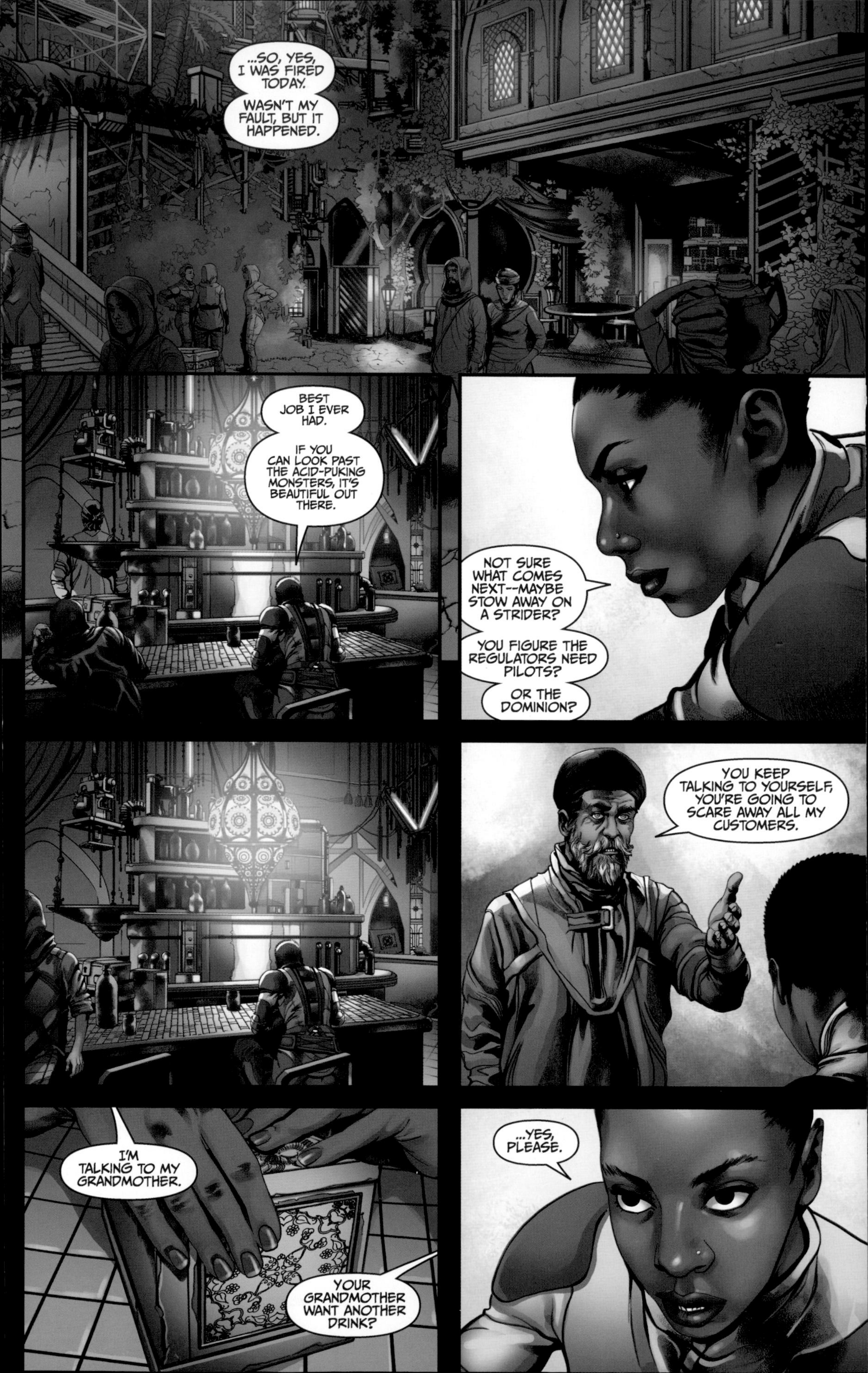
...SO, YES, I WAS FIRED TODAY.
WASN'T MY FAULT, BUT IT HAPPENED.
BEST JOB I EVER HAD.
IF YOU CAN LOOK PAST THE ACID-PUKING MONSTERS, IT'S BEAUTIFUL OUT THERE.
NOT SURE WHAT COMES NEXT--MAYBE STOW AWAY ON A STRIDER?
YOU FIGURE THE REGULATORS NEED PILOTS?
OR THE DOMINION?
YOU KEEP TALKING TO YOURSELF, YOU'RE GOING TO SCARE AWAY ALL MY CUSTOMERS.
I'M TALKING TO MY GRANDMOTHER.
YOUR GRANDMOTHER WANT ANOTHER DRINK?
...YES, PLEASE.

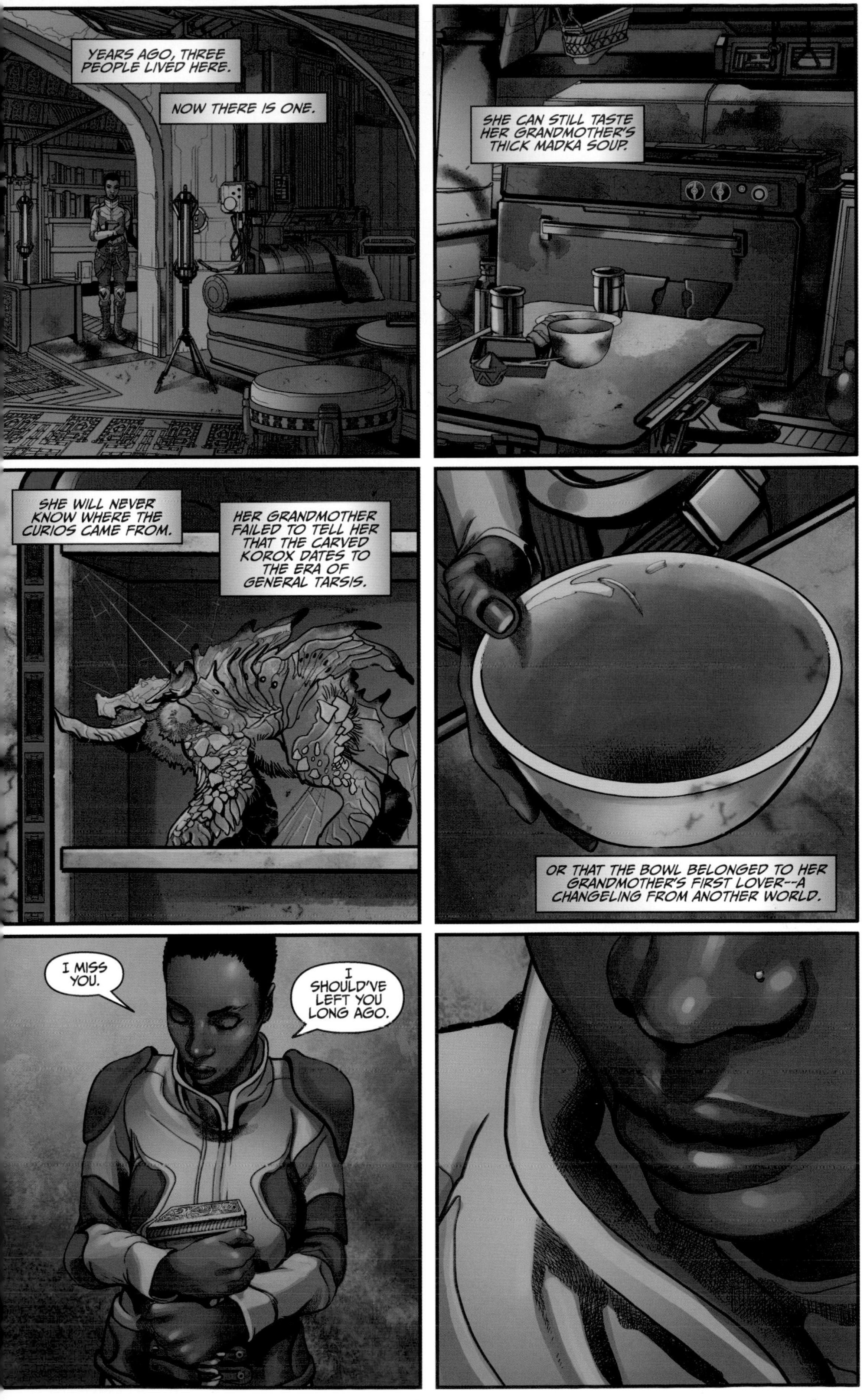

YEARS AGO, THREE PEOPLE LIVED HERE.
NOW THERE IS ONE.
SHE CAN STILL TASTE HER GRANDMOTHER'S THICK MADKA SOUP.
SHE WILL NEVER KNOW WHERE THE CURIOS CAME FROM.
HER GRANDMOTHER FAILED TO TELL HER THAT THE CARVED KOROX DATES TO THE ERA OF GENERAL TARSIS.
OR THAT THE BOWL BELONGED TO HER GRANDMOTHER'S FIRST LOVER--A CHANGELING FROM ANOTHER WORLD.
I MISS YOU.
I SHOULD'VE LEFT YOU LONG AGO.

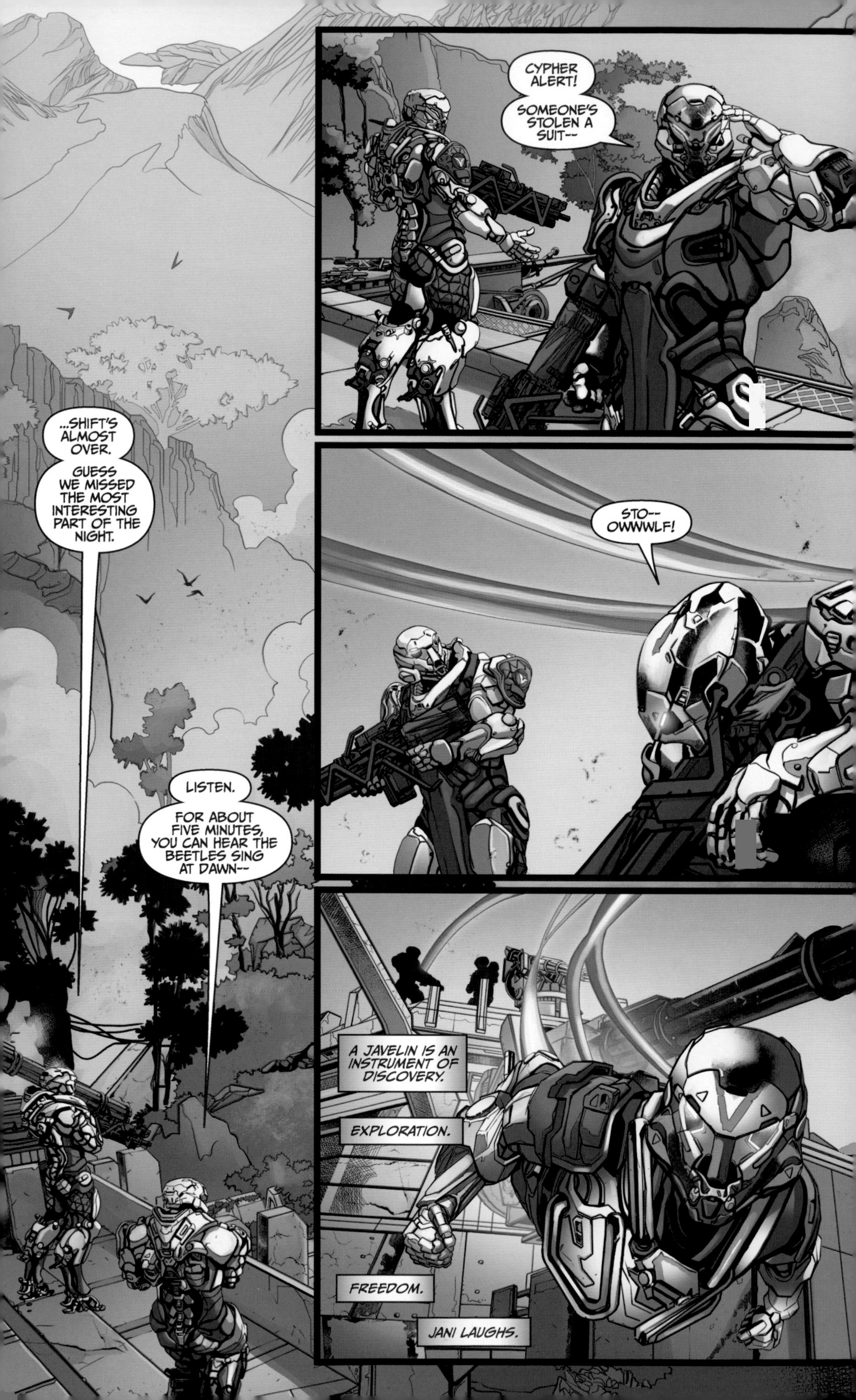
...SHIFT'S ALMOST OVER.
GUESS WE MISSED THE MOST INTERESTING PART OF THE NIGHT.
LISTEN.
FOR ABOUT FIVE MINUTES, YOU CAN HEAR THE BEETLES SING AT DAWN--
CYPHER ALERT!
SOMEONE'S STOLEN A SUIT--
STO-- OWWWLF!
A JAVELIN IS AN INSTRUMENT OF DISCOVERY.
EXPLORATION.
FREEDOM.
JANI LAUGHS.

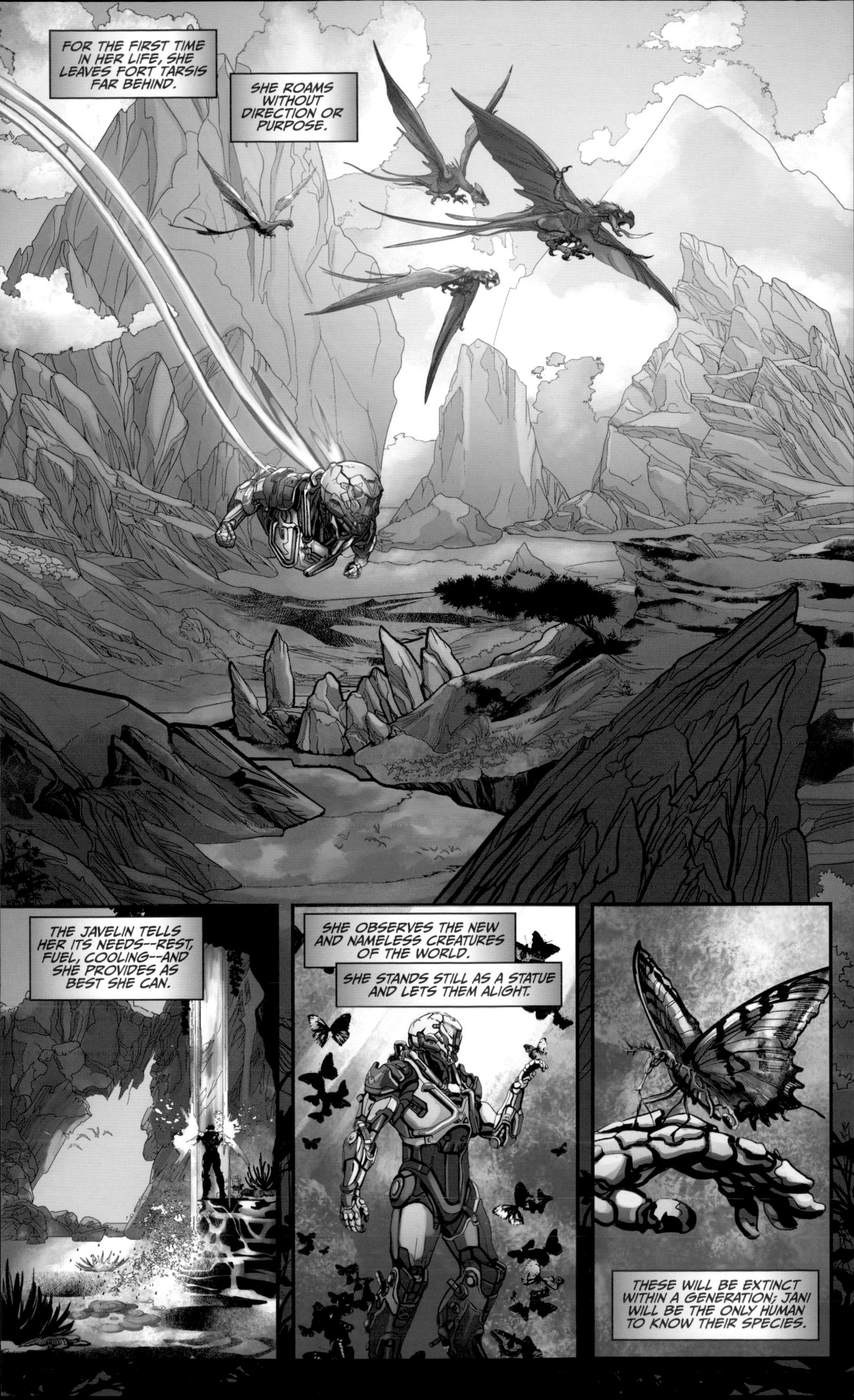
FOR THE FIRST TIME IN HER LIFE, SHE LEAVES FORT TARSIS FAR BEHIND.
SHE ROAMS WITHOUT DIRECTION OR PURPOSE.
THE JAVELIN TELLS HER ITS NEEDS--REST, FUEL, COOLING--AND SHE PROVIDES AS BEST SHE CAN.
SHE OBSERVES THE NEW AND NAMELESS CREATURES OF THE WORLD.
SHE STANDS STILL AS A STATUE AND LETS THEM ALIGHT.
THESE WILL BE EXTINCT WITHIN A GENERATION; JANI WILL BE THE ONLY HUMAN TO KNOW THEIR SPECIES.

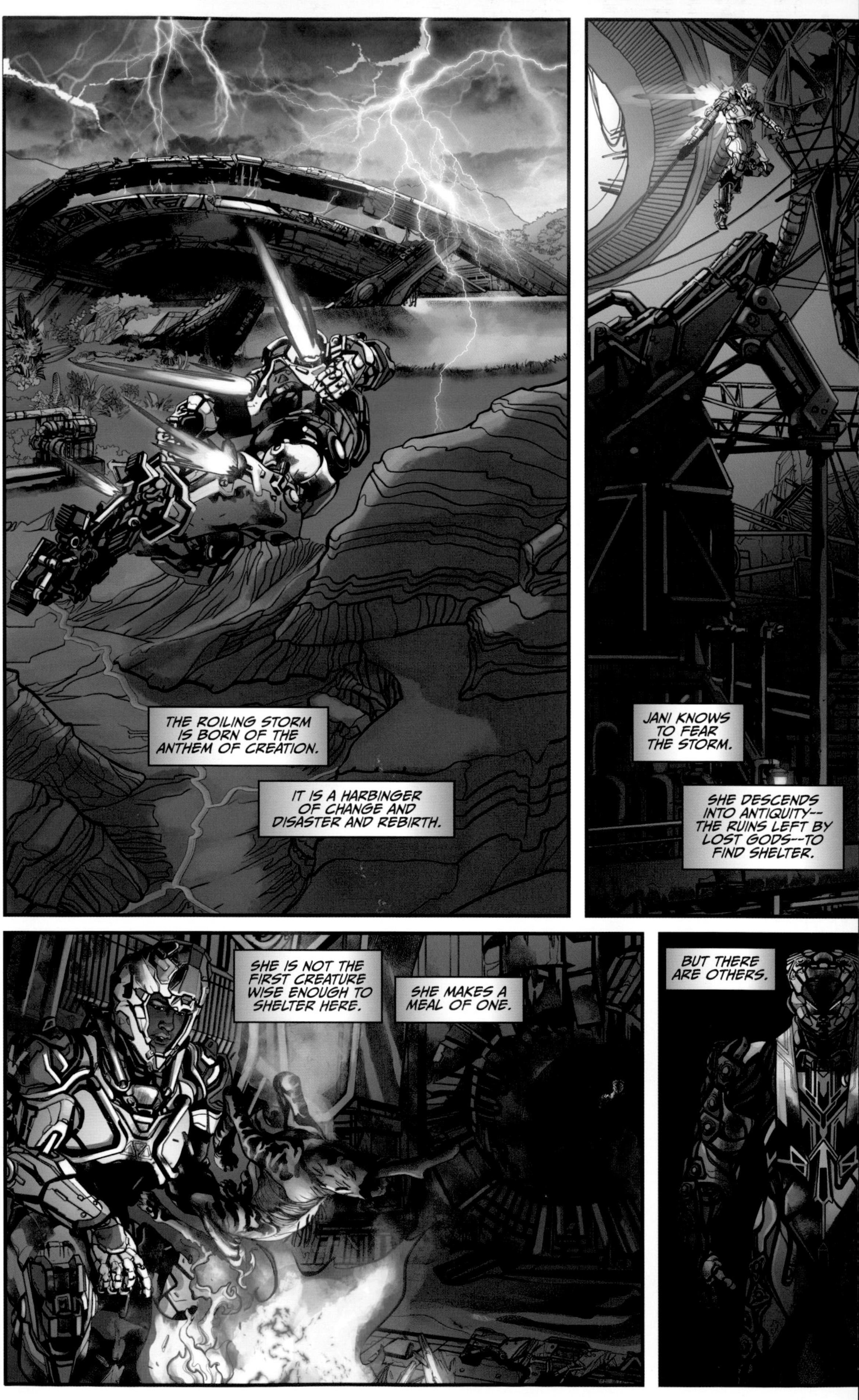
THE ROILING STORM IS BORN OF THE ANTHEM OF CREATION.
IT IS A HARBINGER OF CHANGE AND DISASTER AND REBIRTH.
JANI KNOWS TO FEAR THE STORM.
SHE DESCENDS INTO ANTIQUITY--THE RUINS LEFT BY LOST GODS--TO FIND SHELTER.
SHE IS NOT THE FIRST CREATURE WISE ENOUGH TO SHELTER HERE.
SHE MAKES A MEAL OF ONE.
BUT THERE ARE OTHERS.

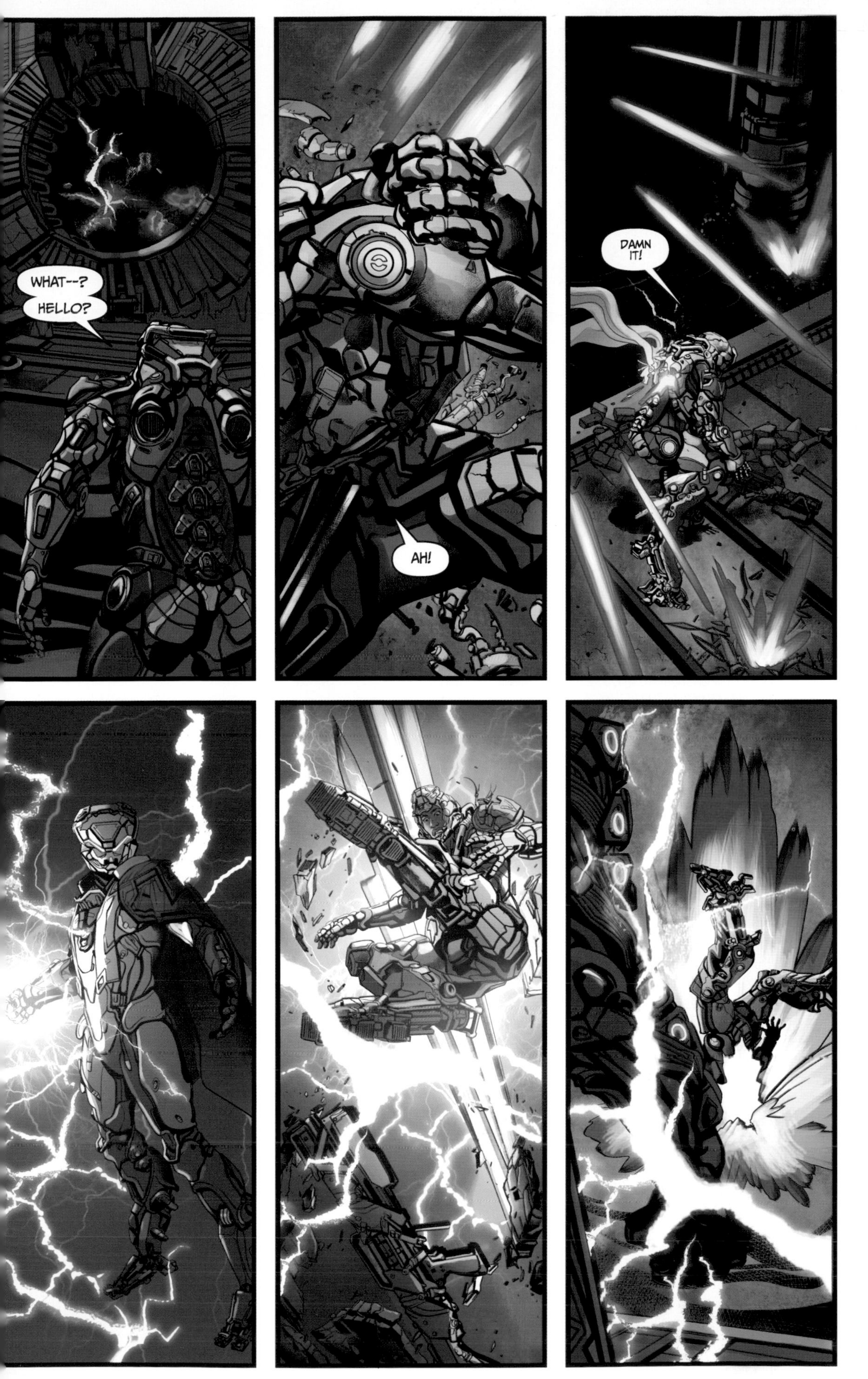
WHAT--?
HELLO?
AH!
DAMN IT!

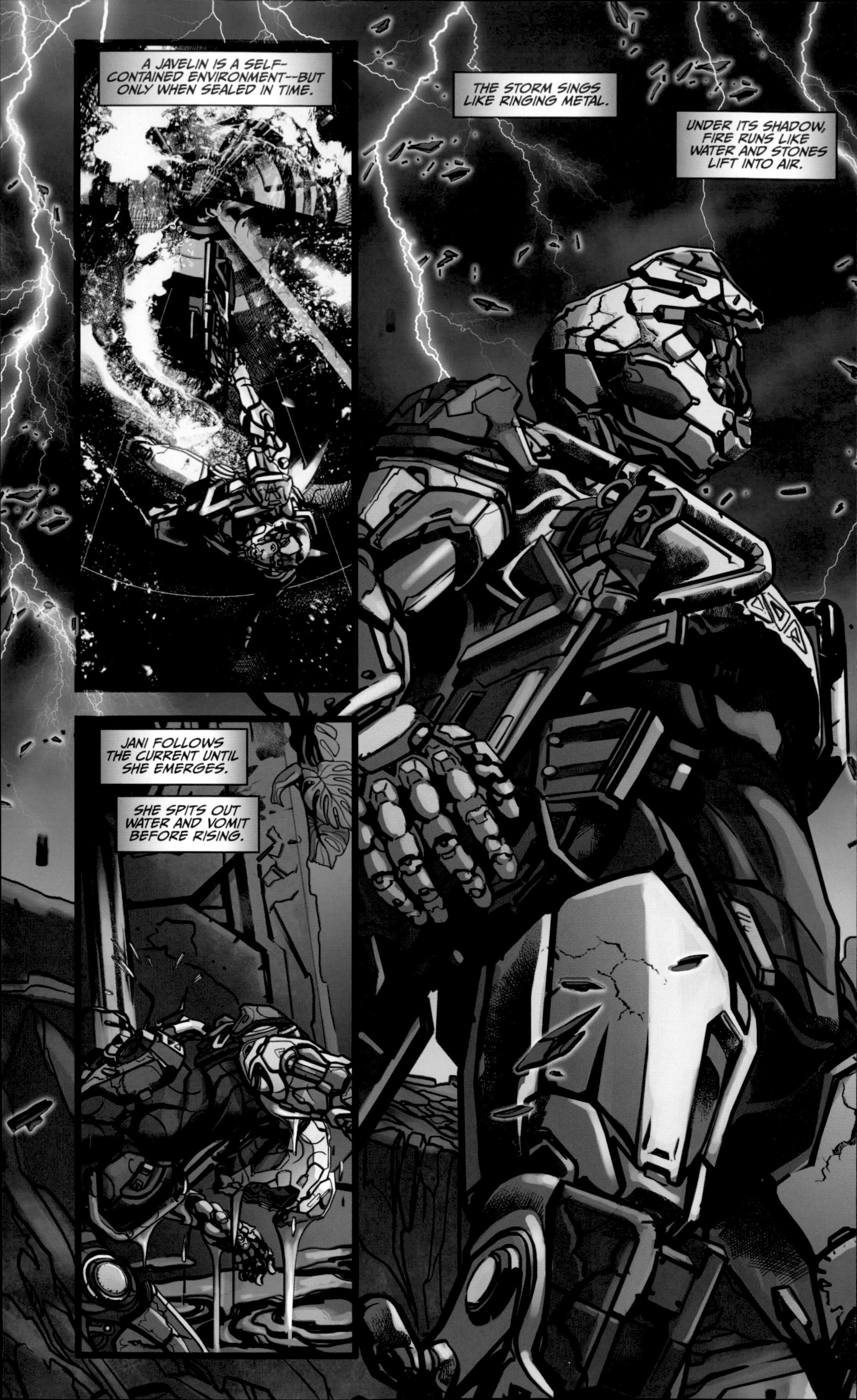
A JAVELIN IS A SELF-CONTAINED ENVIRONMENT--BUT ONLY WHEN SEALED IN TIME.
THE STORM SINGS LIKE RINGING METAL.
UNDER ITS SHADOW, FIRE RUNS LIKE WATER AND STONES LIFT INTO AIR.
JANI FOLLOWS THE CURRENT UNTIL SHE EMERGES.
SHE SPITS OUT WATER AND VOMIT BEFORE RISING.

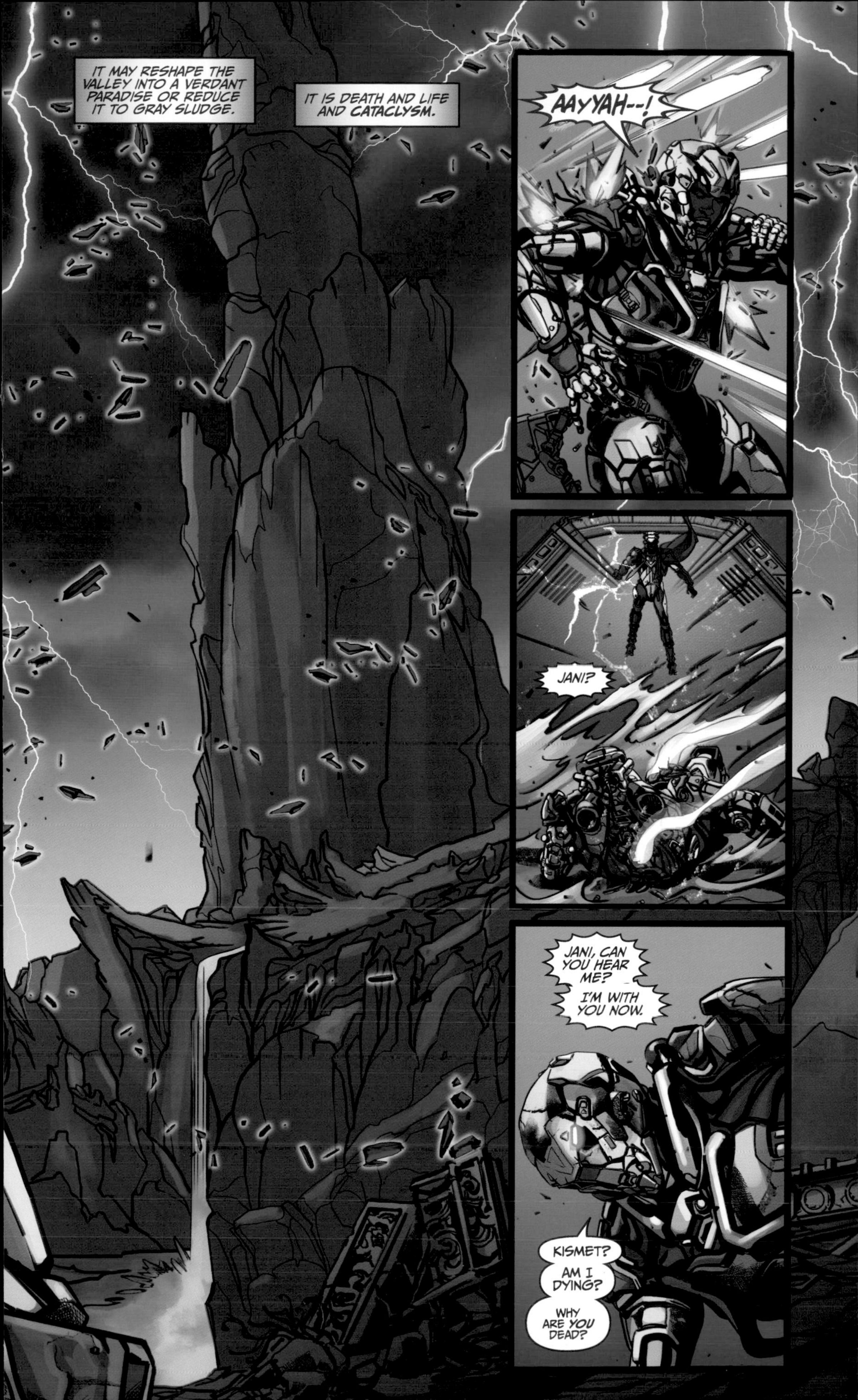

IT MAY RESHAPE THE VALLEY INTO A VERDANT PARADISE OR REDUCE IT TO GRAY SLUDGE.
IT IS DEATH AND LIFE AND CATACLYSM.
AAYYAH--!
JANI?
JANI, CAN YOU HEAR ME?
I'M WITH YOU NOW.
KISMET?
AM I DYING?
WHY ARE YOU DEAD?

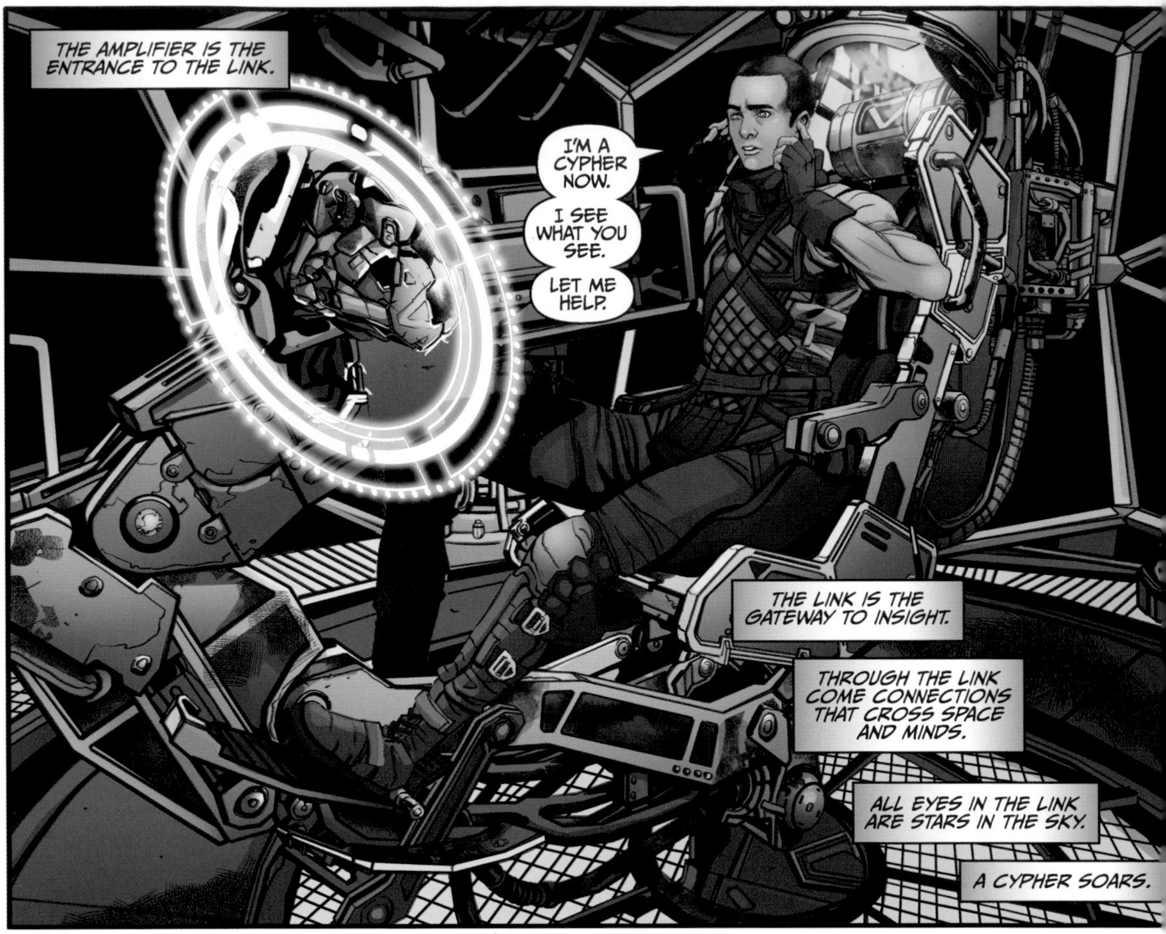
THE AMPLIFIER IS THE ENTRANCE TO THE LINK.
I'M A CYPHER NOW.
I SEE WHAT YOU SEE.
LET ME HELP.
THE LINK IS THE GATEWAY TO INSIGHT.
THROUGH THE LINK COME CONNECTIONS THAT CROSS SPACE AND MINDS.
ALL EYES IN THE LINK ARE STARS IN THE SKY.
A CYPHER SOARS.
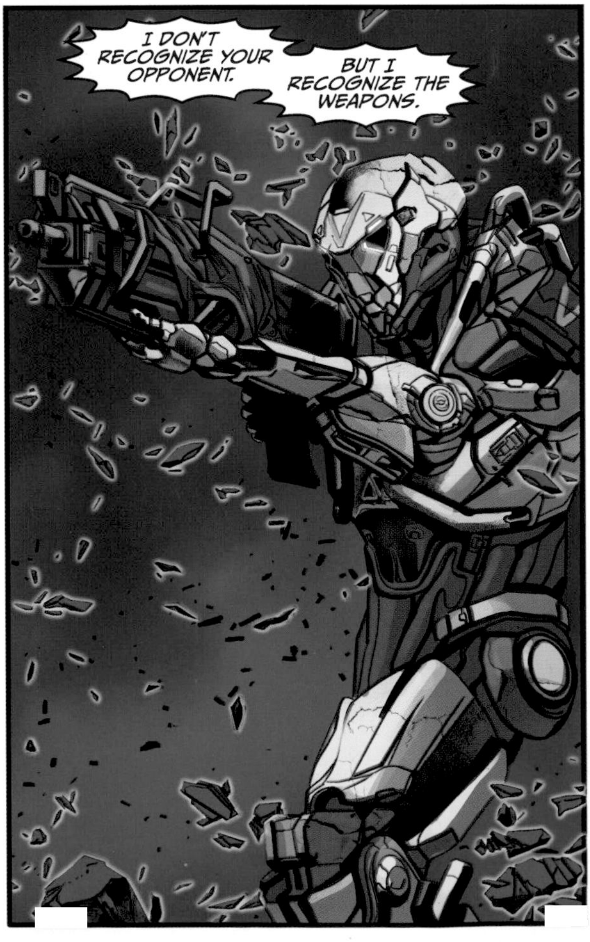
I DON'T RECOGNIZE YOUR OPPONENT.
BUT I RECOGNIZE THE WEAPONS.
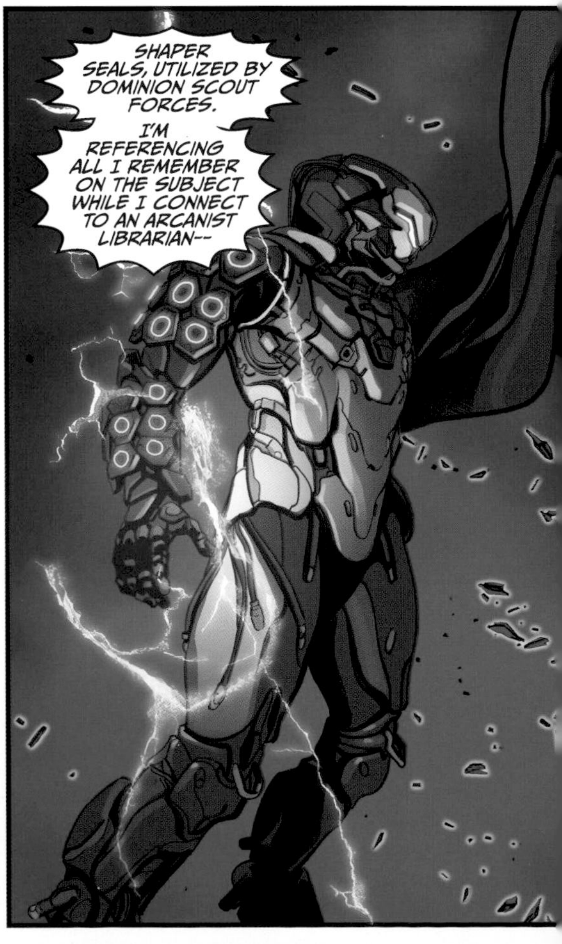
SHAPER SEALS, UTILIZED BY DOMINION SCOUT FORCES.
I'M REFERENCING ALL I REMEMBER ON THE SUBJECT WHILE I CONNECT TO AN ARCANIST LIBRARIAN--

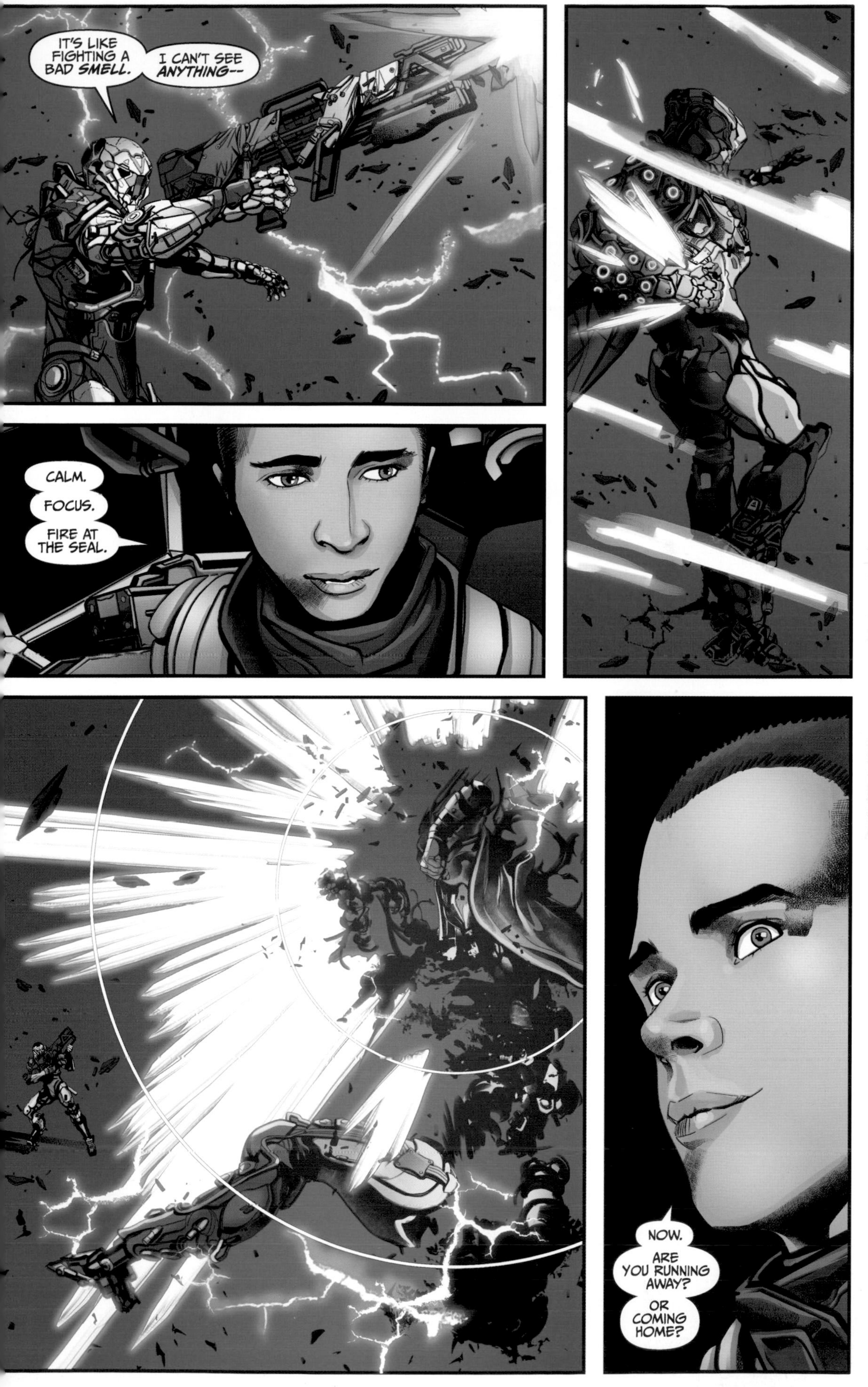
IT'S LIKE FIGHTING A BAD SMELL.
I CAN'T SEE ANYTHING--
CALM.
FOCUS.
FIRE AT THE SEAL.
NOW.
ARE YOU RUNNING AWAY?
OR COMING HOME?

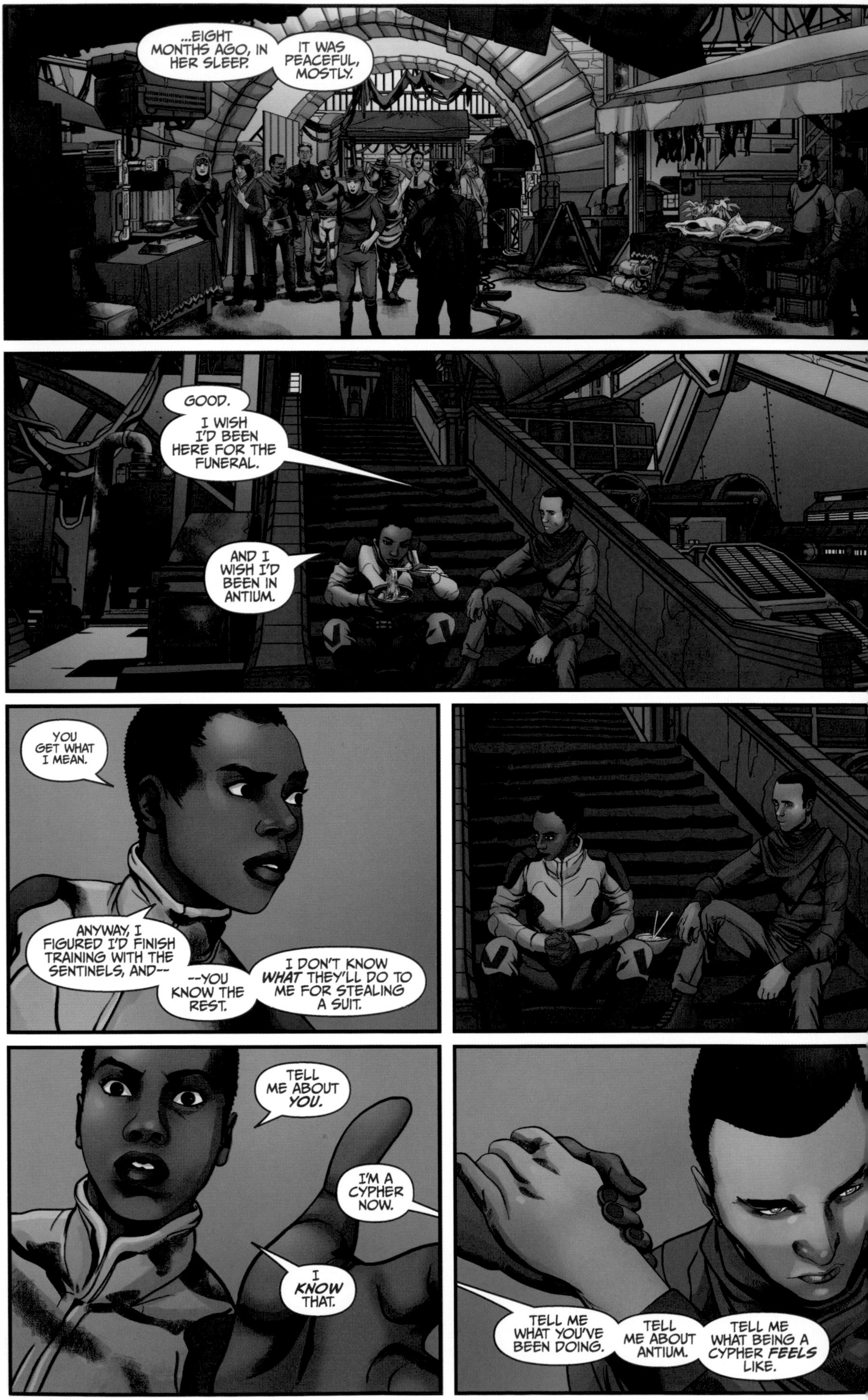
...EIGHT MONTHS AGO, IN HER SLEEP.
IT WAS PEACEFUL, MOSTLY.
GOOD.
I WISH I'D BEEN HERE FOR THE FUNERAL.
AND I WISH I'D BEEN IN ANTIUM.
YOU GET WHAT I MEAN.
ANYWAY, I FIGURED I'D FINISH TRAINING WITH THE SENTINELS, AND--
--YOU KNOW THE REST.
I DON'T KNOW *WHAT* THEY'LL DO TO ME FOR STEALING A SUIT.
TELL ME ABOUT *YOU.*
I'M A CYPHER NOW.
I *KNOW* THAT.
TELL ME WHAT YOU'VE BEEN DOING.
TELL ME ABOUT ANTIUM.
TELL ME WHAT BEING A CYPHER *FEELS* LIKE.

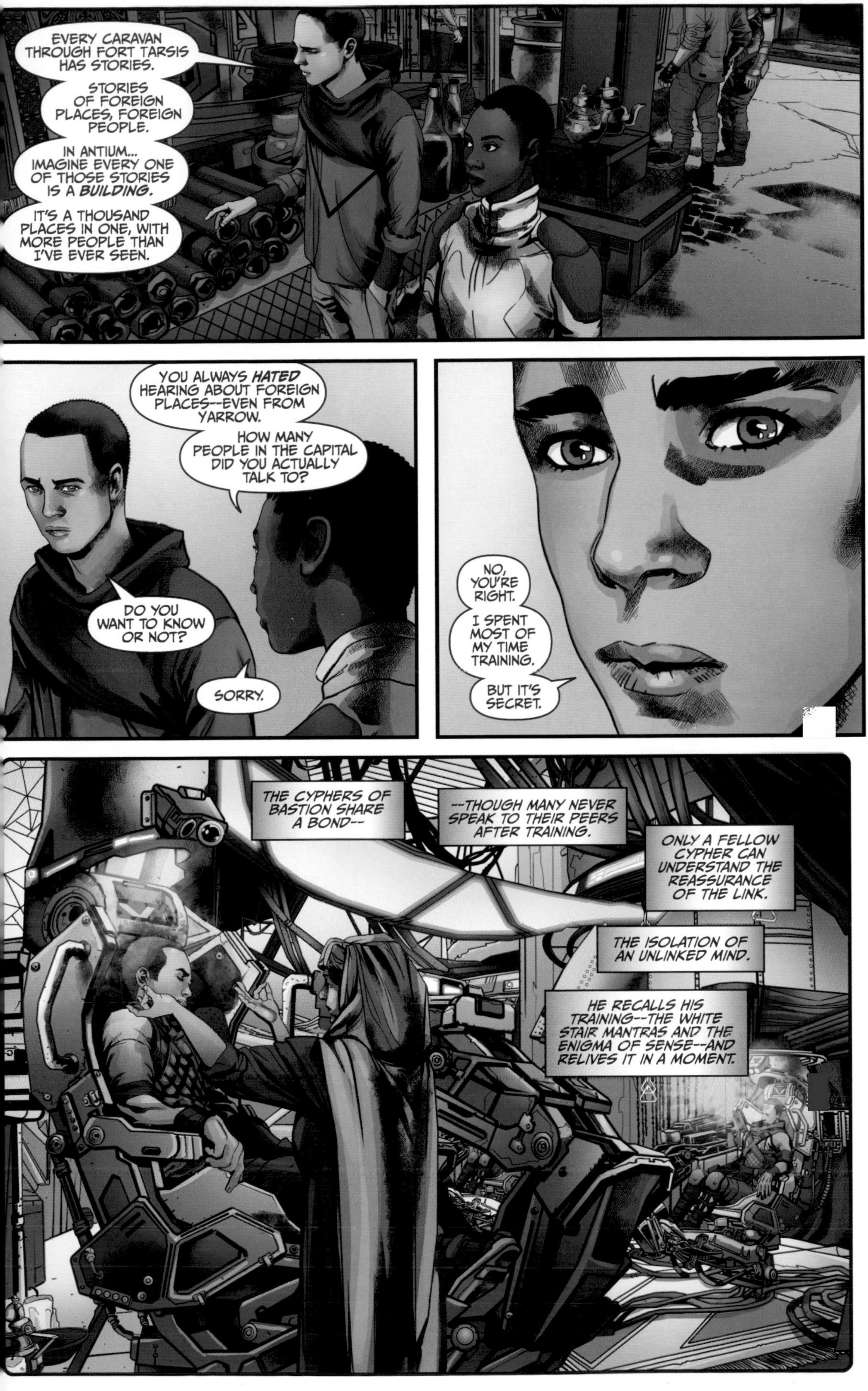
EVERY CARAVAN THROUGH FORT TARSIS HAS STORIES.
STORIES OF FOREIGN PLACES, FOREIGN PEOPLE.
IN ANTIUM... IMAGINE EVERY ONE OF THOSE STORIES IS A *BUILDING*.
IT'S A THOUSAND PLACES IN ONE, WITH MORE PEOPLE THAN I'VE EVER SEEN.
YOU ALWAYS *HATED* HEARING ABOUT FOREIGN PLACES--EVEN FROM YARROW.
HOW MANY PEOPLE IN THE CAPITAL DID YOU ACTUALLY TALK TO?
DO YOU WANT TO KNOW OR NOT?
SORRY.
NO, YOU'RE RIGHT.
I SPENT MOST OF MY TIME TRAINING.
BUT IT'S SECRET.
THE CYPHERS OF BASTION SHARE A BOND--
--THOUGH MANY NEVER SPEAK TO THEIR PEERS AFTER TRAINING.
ONLY A FELLOW CYPHER CAN UNDERSTAND THE REASSURANCE OF THE LINK.
THE ISOLATION OF AN UNLINKED MIND.
HE RECALLS HIS TRAINING--THE WHITE STAIR MANTRAS AND THE ENIGMA OF SENSE--AND RELIVES IT IN A MOMENT.

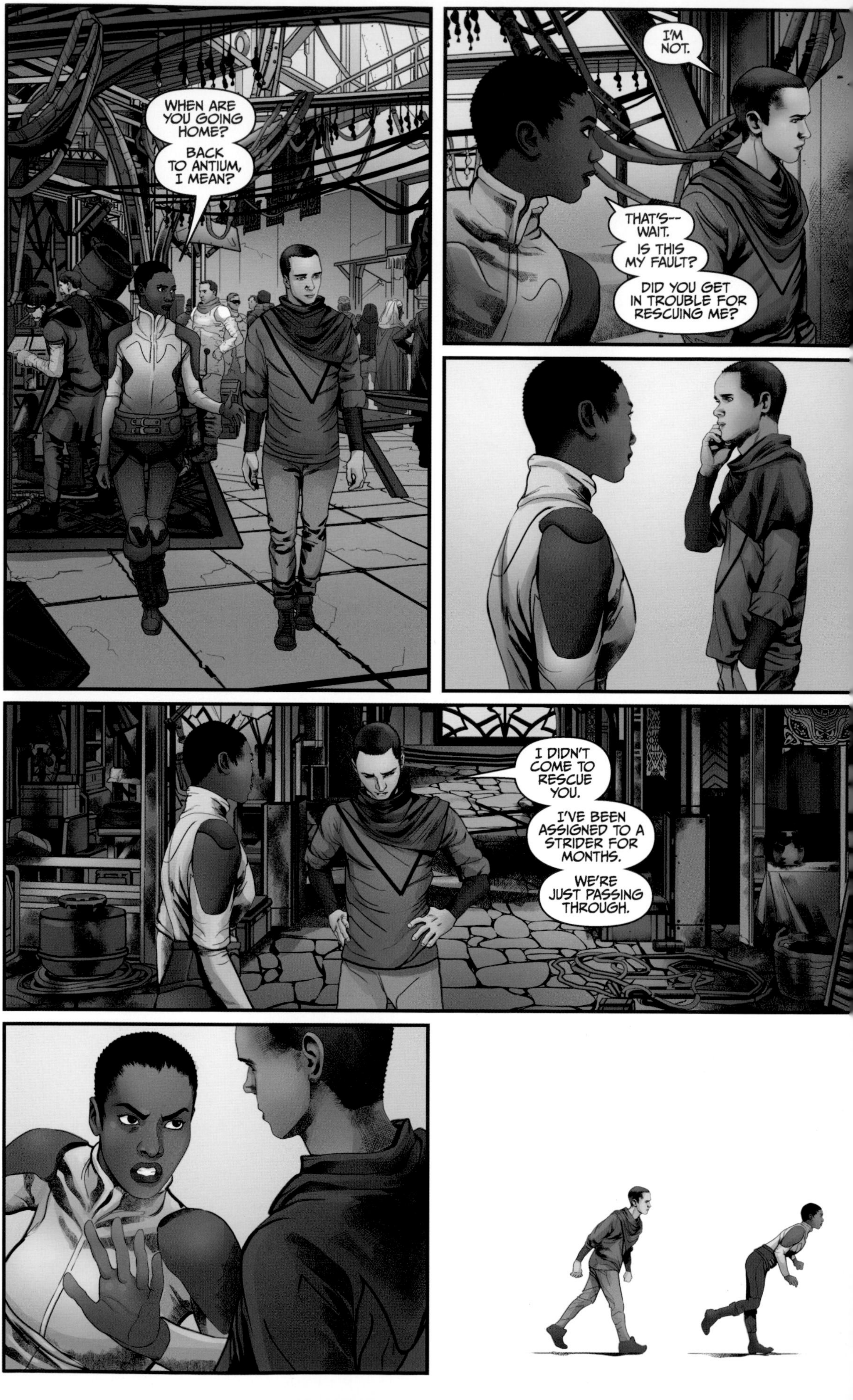
WHEN ARE YOU GOING HOME?
BACK TO ANTIUM, I MEAN?
I'M NOT.
THAT'S-- WAIT.
IS THIS MY FAULT?
DID YOU GET IN TROUBLE FOR RESCUING ME?
I DIDN'T COME TO RESCUE YOU.
I'VE BEEN ASSIGNED TO A STRIDER FOR MONTHS.
WE'RE JUST PASSING THROUGH.

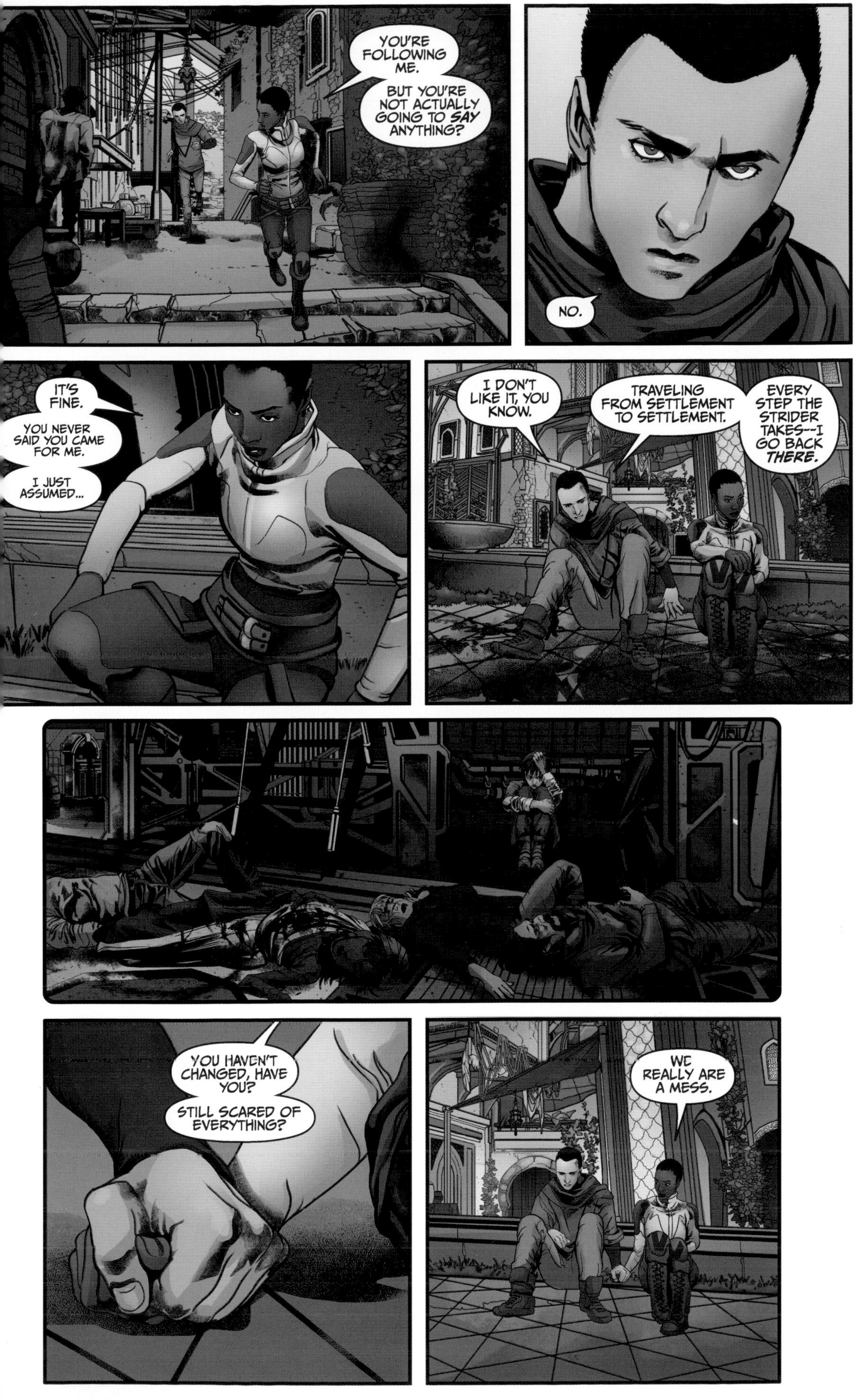
YOU'RE FOLLOWING ME.
BUT YOU'RE NOT ACTUALLY GOING TO SAY ANYTHING?
NO.
IT'S FINE.
YOU NEVER SAID YOU CAME FOR ME.
I JUST ASSUMED...
I DON'T LIKE IT, YOU KNOW.
TRAVELING FROM SETTLEMENT TO SETTLEMENT.
EVERY STEP THE STRIDER TAKES--I GO BACK THERE.
YOU HAVEN'T CHANGED, HAVE YOU?
STILL SCARED OF EVERYTHING?
WE REALLY ARE A MESS.

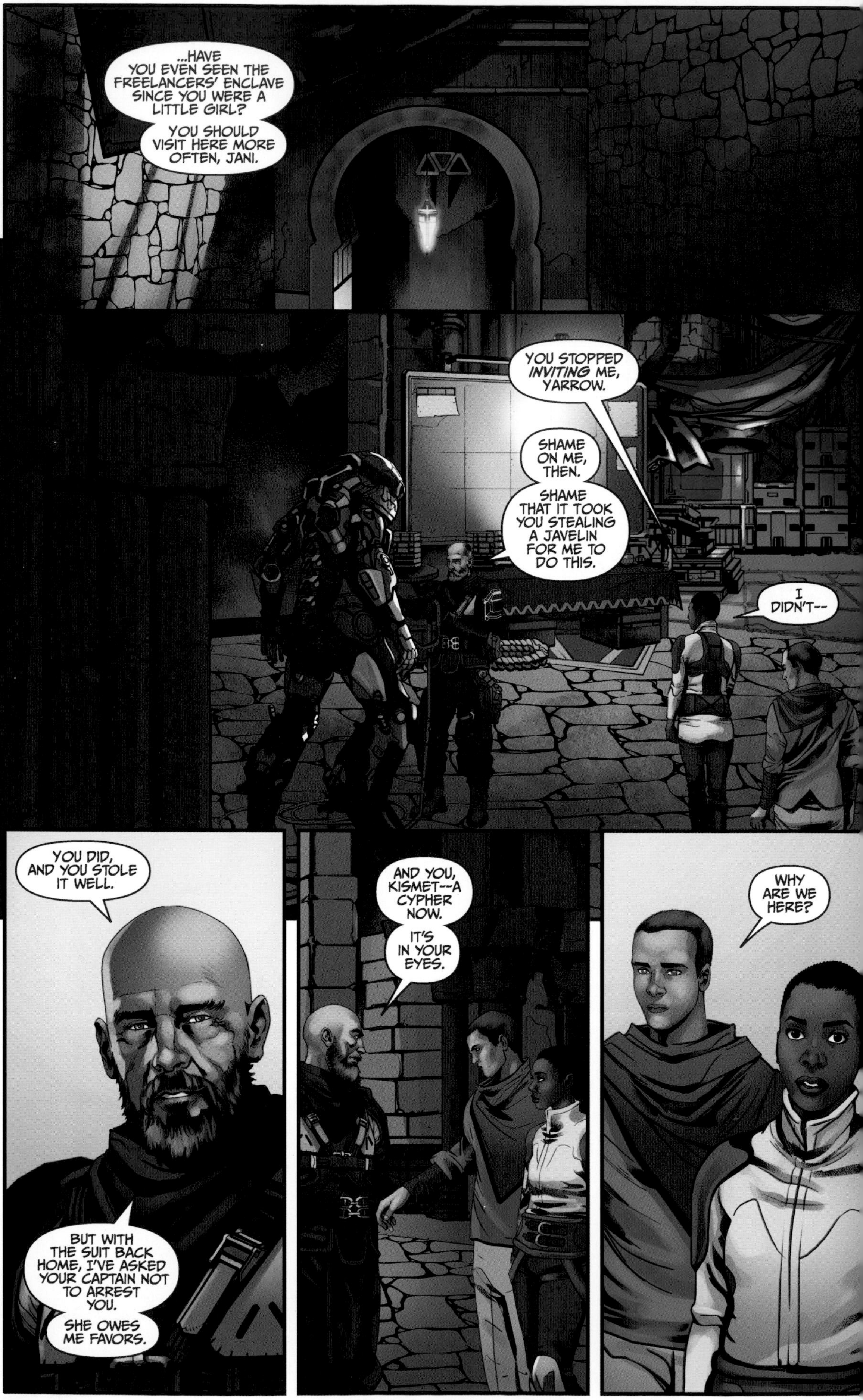
...HAVE YOU EVEN SEEN THE FREELANCERS' ENCLAVE SINCE YOU WERE A LITTLE GIRL?
YOU SHOULD VISIT HERE MORE OFTEN, JANI.
YOU STOPPED *INVITING* ME, YARROW.
SHAME ON ME, THEN.
SHAME THAT IT TOOK YOU STEALING A JAVELIN FOR ME TO DO THIS.
I DIDN'T--
YOU DID, AND YOU STOLE IT WELL.
BUT WITH THE SUIT BACK HOME, I'VE ASKED YOUR CAPTAIN NOT TO ARREST YOU.
SHE OWES ME FAVORS.
AND YOU, KISMET--A CYPHER NOW.
IT'S IN YOUR EYES.
WHY ARE WE HERE?

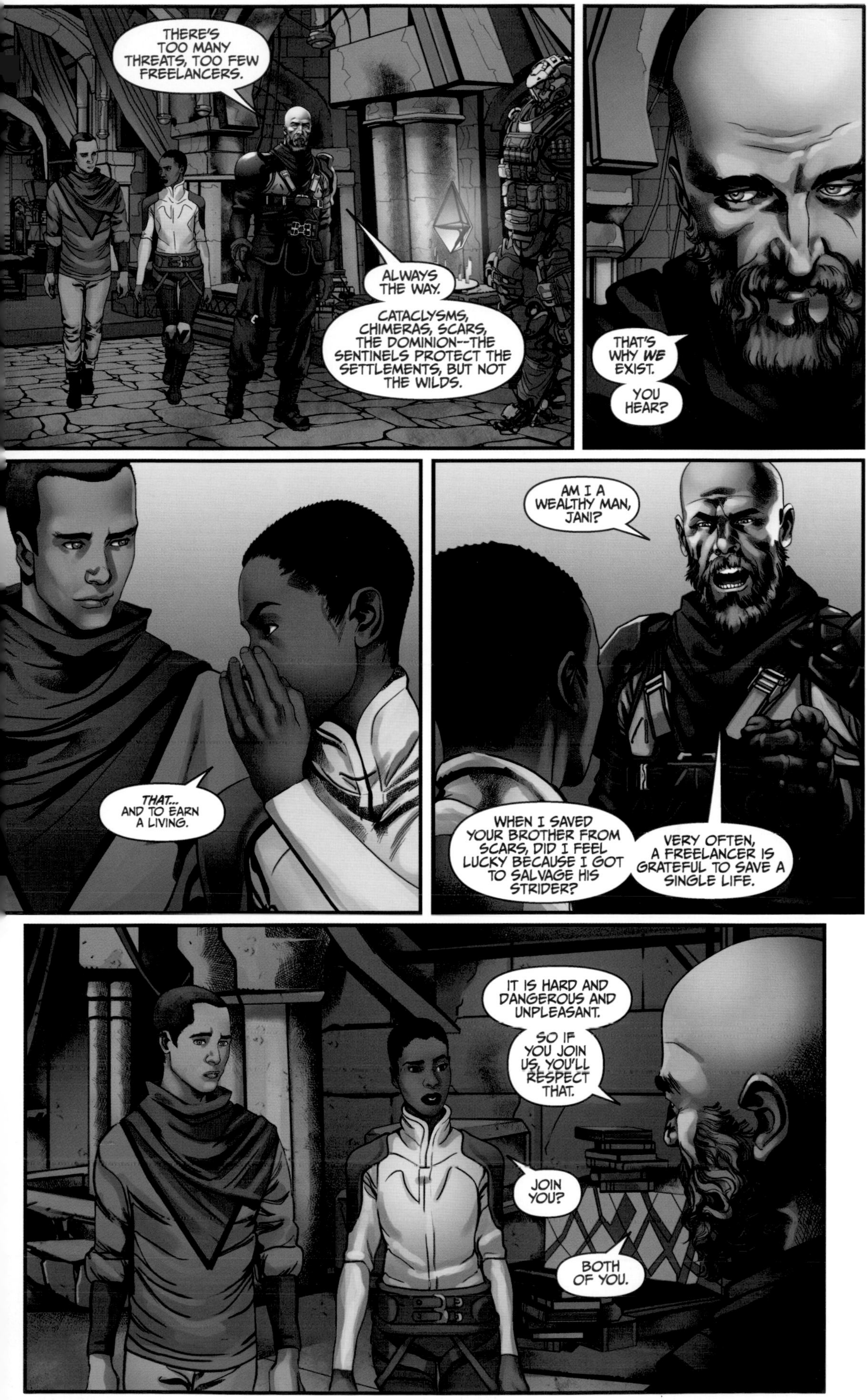
THERE'S TOO MANY THREATS, TOO FEW FREELANCERS.
ALWAYS THE WAY.
CATACLYSMS, CHIMERAS, SCARS, THE DOMINION--THE SENTINELS PROTECT THE SETTLEMENTS, BUT NOT THE WILDS.
THAT'S WHY *WE* EXIST.
YOU HEAR?
THAT... AND TO EARN A LIVING.
AM I A WEALTHY MAN, JANI?
VERY OFTEN, A FREELANCER IS GRATEFUL TO SAVE A SINGLE LIFE.
WHEN I SAVED YOUR BROTHER FROM SCARS, DID I FEEL LUCKY BECAUSE I GOT TO SALVAGE HIS STRIDER?
IT IS HARD AND DANGEROUS AND UNPLEASANT.
SO IF YOU JOIN US, YOU'LL RESPECT THAT.
JOIN YOU?
BOTH OF YOU.

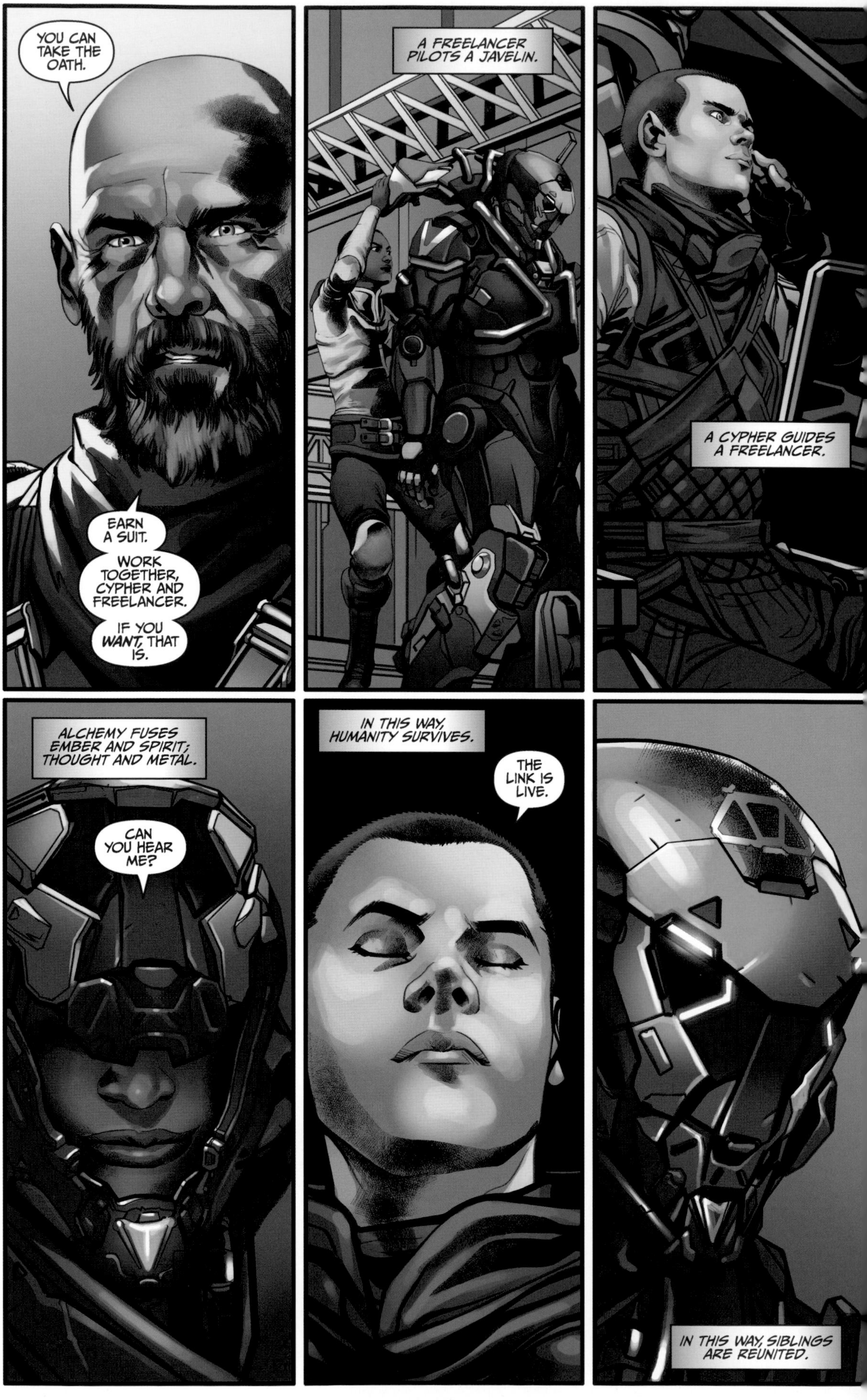
YOU CAN TAKE THE OATH.
EARN A SUIT.
WORK TOGETHER, CYPHER AND FREELANCER.
IF YOU WANT, THAT IS.
A FREELANCER PILOTS A JAVELIN.
A CYPHER GUIDES A FREELANCER.
ALCHEMY FUSES EMBER AND SPIRIT; THOUGHT AND METAL.
CAN YOU HEAR ME?
IN THIS WAY, HUMANITY SURVIVES.
THE LINK IS LIVE.
IN THIS WAY, SIBLINGS ARE REUNITED.

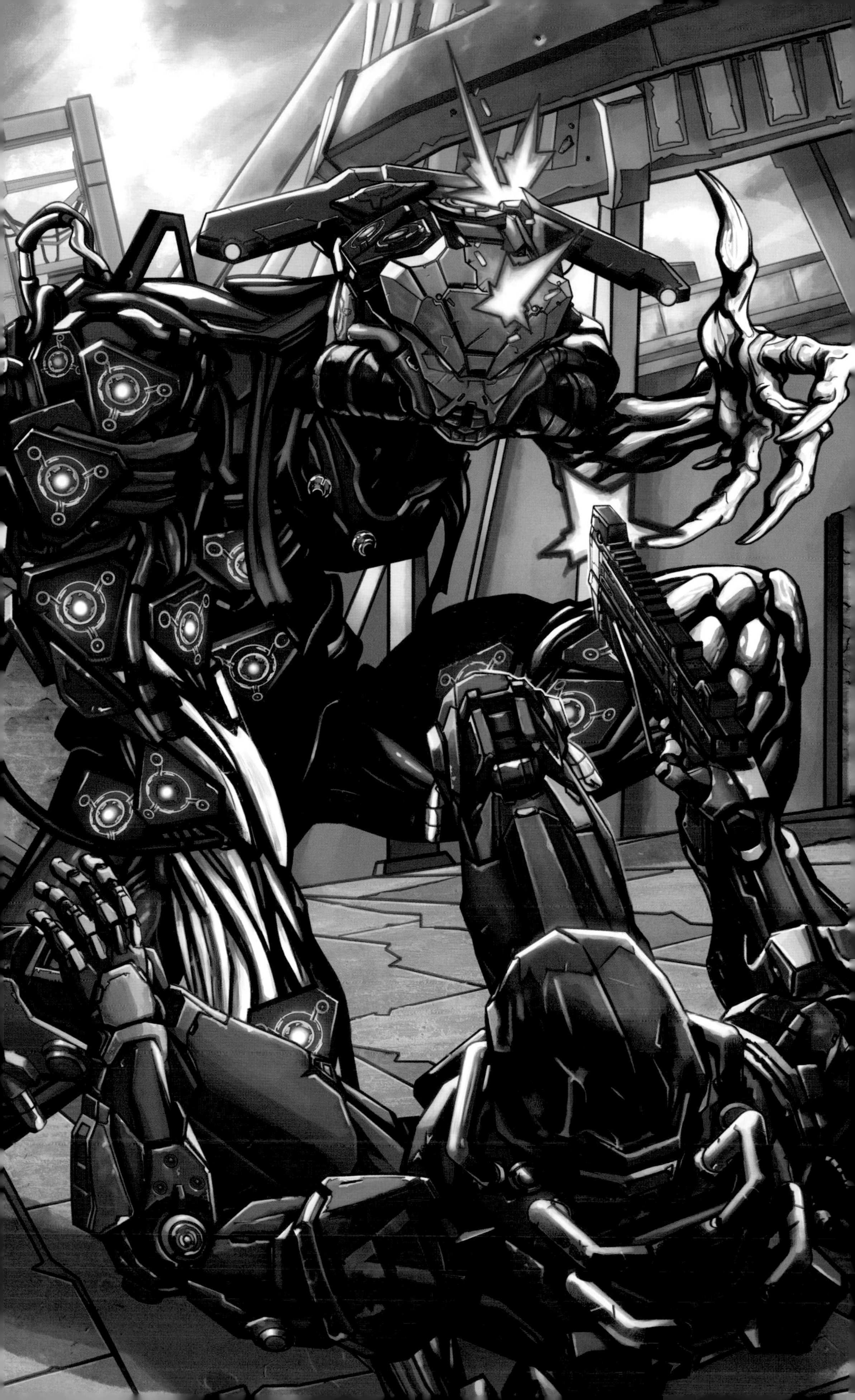

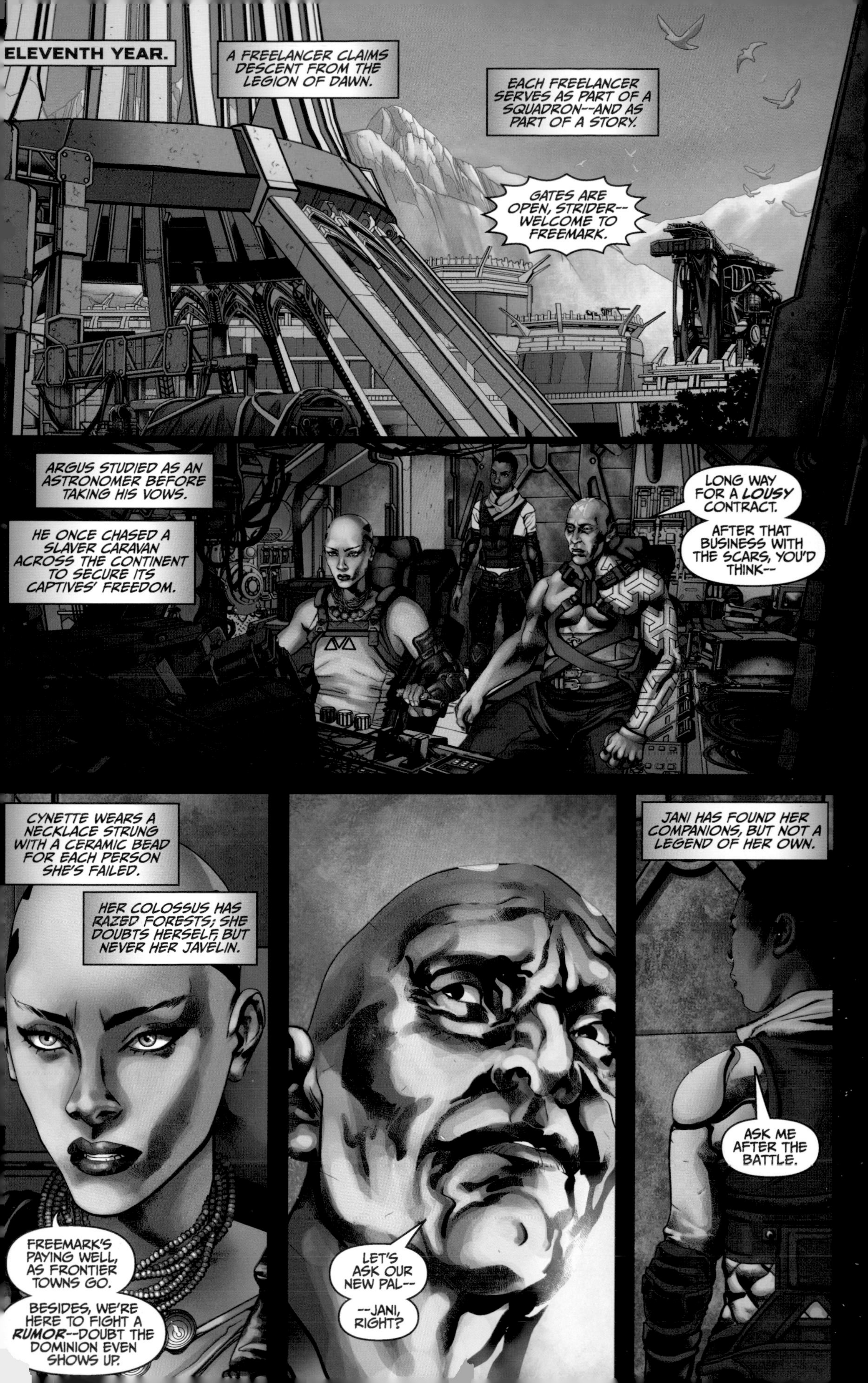

ELEVENTH YEAR.
A FREELANCER CLAIMS DESCENT FROM THE LEGION OF DAWN.
EACH FREELANCER SERVES AS PART OF A SQUADRON--AND AS PART OF A STORY.
GATES ARE OPEN, STRIDER--WELCOME TO FREEMARK.
ARGUS STUDIED AS AN ASTRONOMER BEFORE TAKING HIS VOWS.
HE ONCE CHASED A SLAVER CARAVAN ACROSS THE CONTINENT TO SECURE ITS CAPTIVES' FREEDOM.
LONG WAY FOR A LOUSY CONTRACT.
AFTER THAT BUSINESS WITH THE SCARS, YOU'D THINK--
CYNETTE WEARS A NECKLACE STRUNG WITH A CERAMIC BEAD FOR EACH PERSON SHE'S FAILED.
HER COLOSSUS HAS RAZED FORESTS; SHE DOUBTS HERSELF, BUT NEVER HER JAVELIN.
FREEMARK'S PAYING WELL, AS FRONTIER TOWNS GO.
BESIDES, WE'RE HERE TO FIGHT A RUMOR--DOUBT THE DOMINION EVEN SHOWS UP.
LET'S ASK OUR NEW PAL--
--JANI, RIGHT?
JANI HAS FOUND HER COMPANIONS, BUT NOT A LEGEND OF HER OWN.
ASK ME AFTER THE BATTLE.

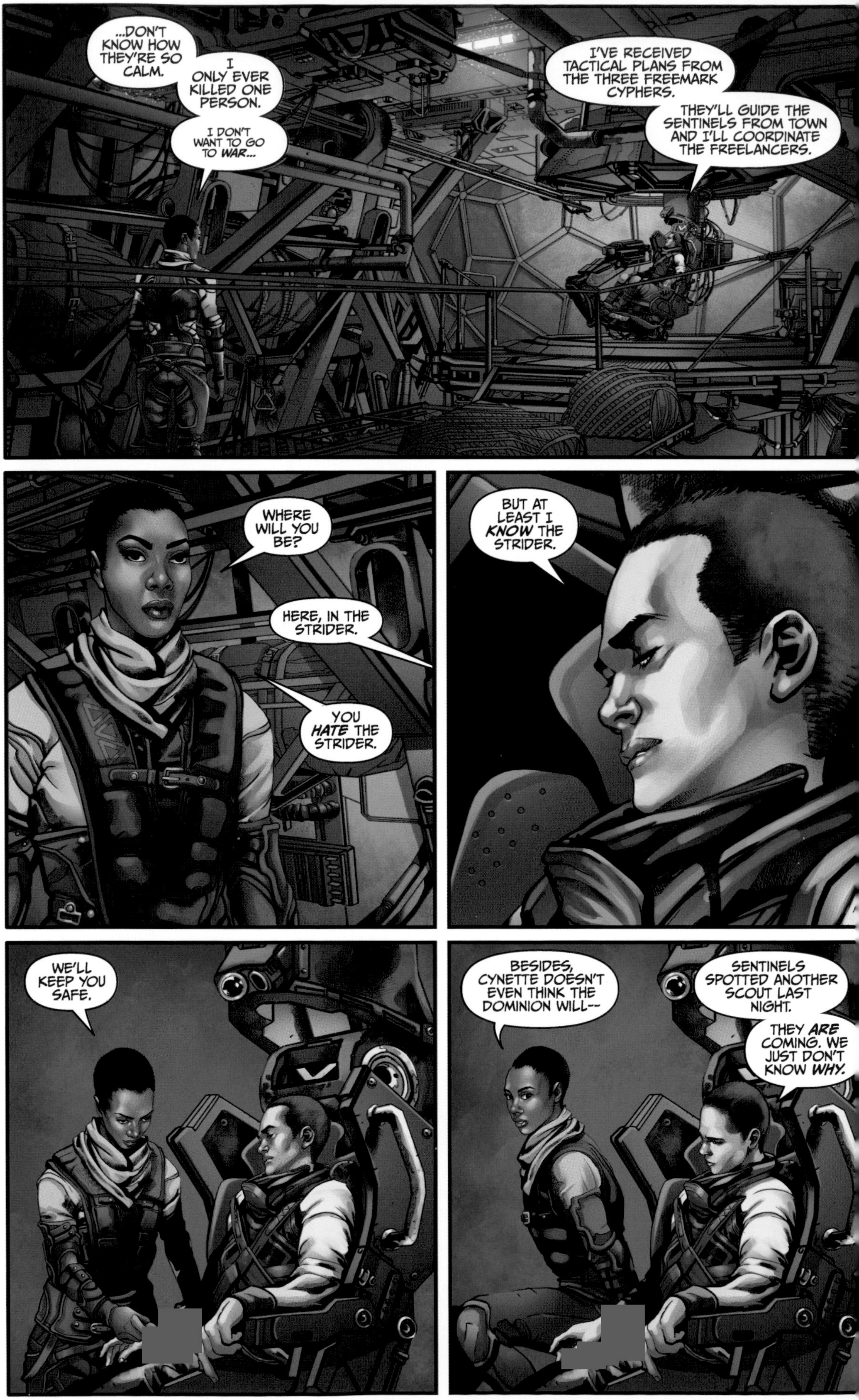

...DON'T KNOW HOW THEY'RE SO CALM.
I ONLY EVER KILLED ONE PERSON.
I DON'T WANT TO GO TO WAR...
I'VE RECEIVED TACTICAL PLANS FROM THE THREE FREEMARK CYPHERS.
THEY'LL GUIDE THE SENTINELS FROM TOWN AND I'LL COORDINATE THE FREELANCERS.
WHERE WILL YOU BE?
HERE, IN THE STRIDER.
YOU HATE THE STRIDER.
BUT AT LEAST I KNOW THE STRIDER.
WE'LL KEEP YOU SAFE.
BESIDES, CYNETTE DOESN'T EVEN THINK THE DOMINION WILL--
SENTINELS SPOTTED ANOTHER SCOUT LAST NIGHT.
THEY ARE COMING. WE JUST DON'T KNOW WHY.

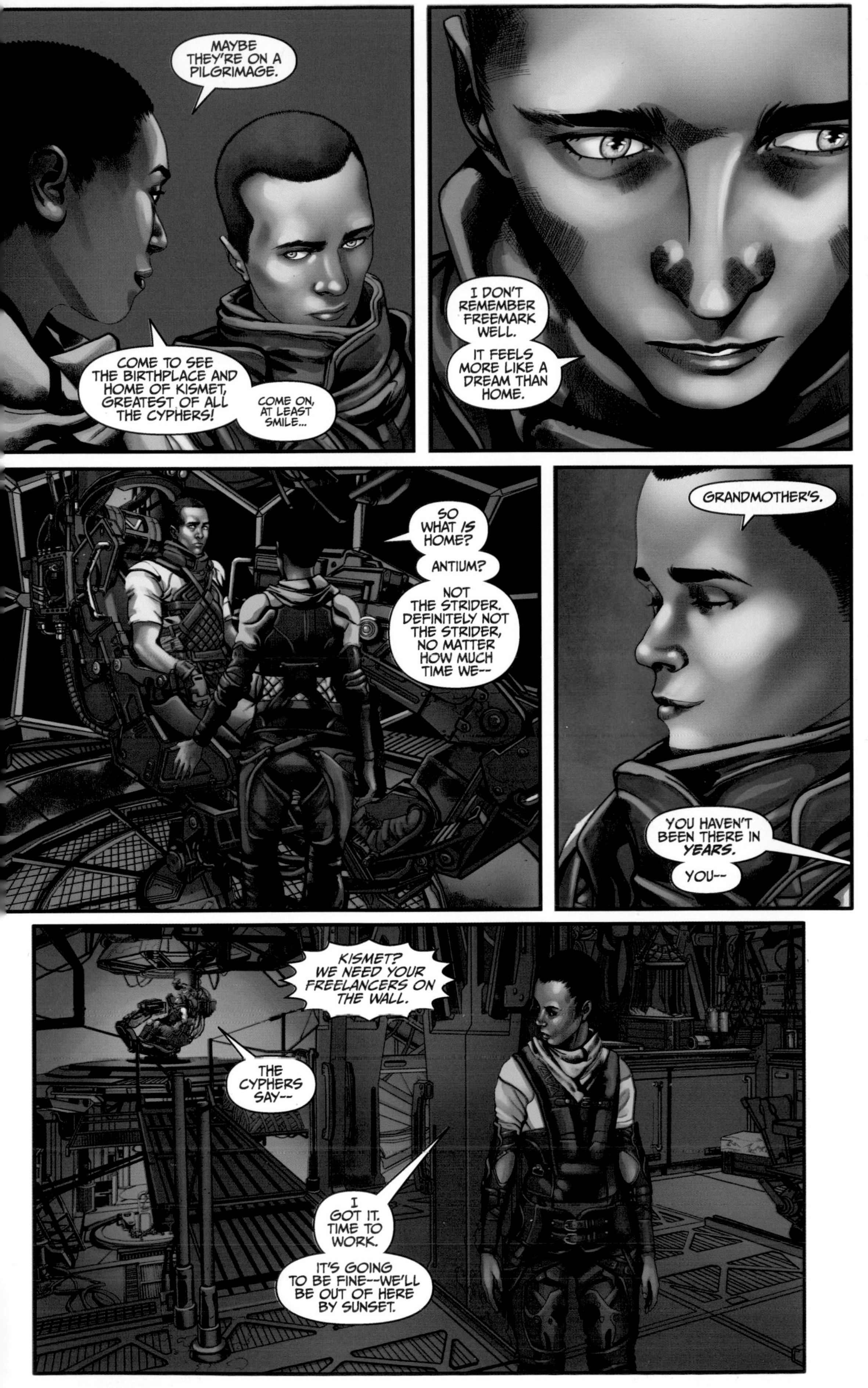
MAYBE THEY'RE ON A PILGRIMAGE.
COME TO SEE THE BIRTHPLACE AND HOME OF KISMET, GREATEST OF ALL THE CYPHERS!
COME ON, AT LEAST SMILE...
I DON'T REMEMBER FREEMARK WELL.
IT FEELS MORE LIKE A DREAM THAN HOME.
SO WHAT *IS* HOME?
ANTIUM?
NOT THE STRIDER. DEFINITELY NOT THE STRIDER, NO MATTER HOW MUCH TIME WE--
GRANDMOTHER'S.
YOU HAVEN'T BEEN THERE IN *YEARS.*
YOU--
KISMET? WE NEED YOUR FREELANCERS ON THE WALL.
THE CYPHERS SAY--
I GOT IT. TIME TO WORK.
IT'S GOING TO BE FINE--WE'LL BE OUT OF HERE BY SUNSET.

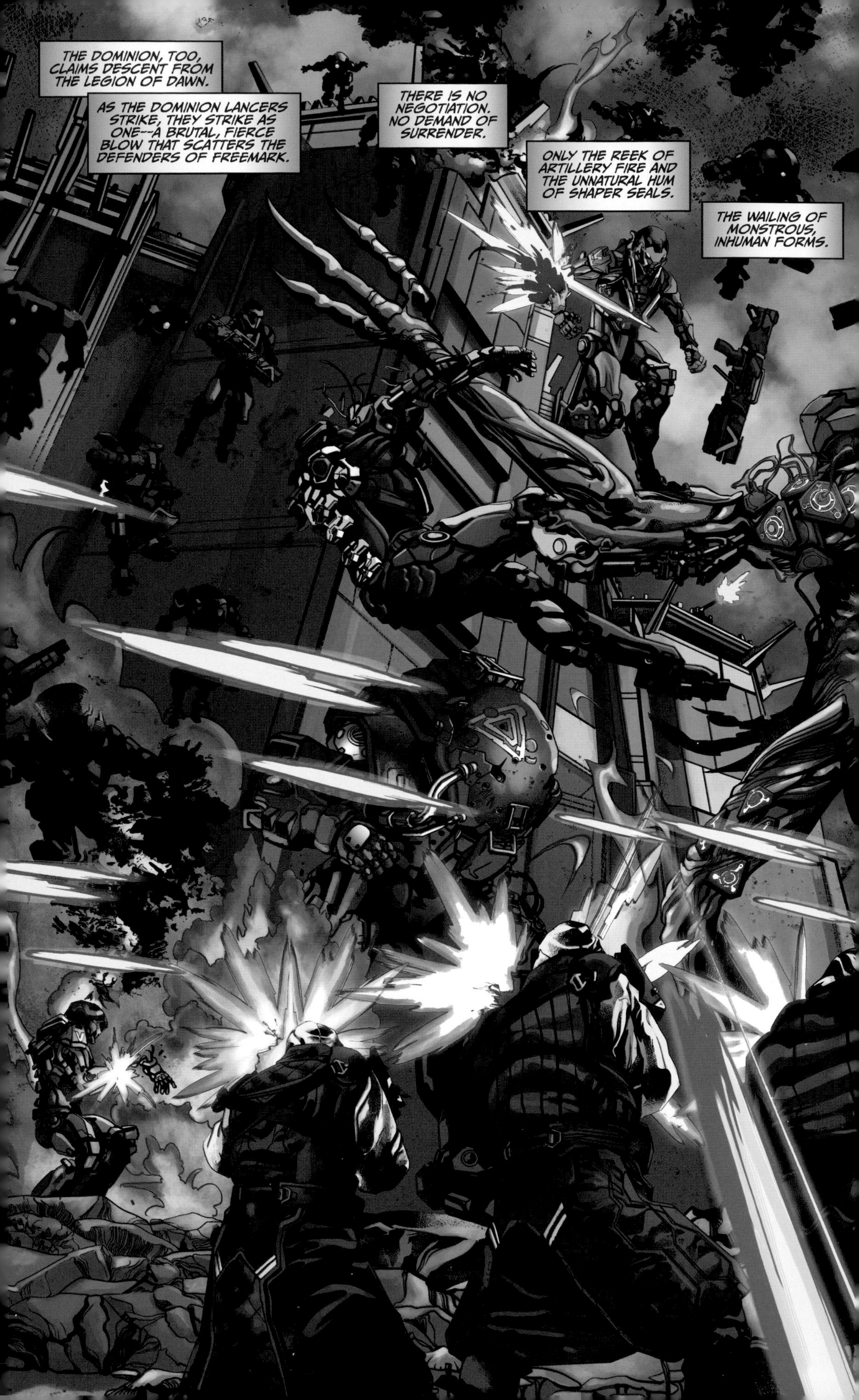
THE DOMINION, TOO, CLAIMS DESCENT FROM THE LEGION OF DAWN.
AS THE DOMINION LANCERS STRIKE, THEY STRIKE AS ONE--A BRUTAL, FIERCE BLOW THAT SCATTERS THE DEFENDERS OF FREEMARK.
THERE IS NO NEGOTIATION. NO DEMAND OF SURRENDER.
ONLY THE REEK OF ARTILLERY FIRE AND THE UNNATURAL HUM OF SHAPER SEALS.
THE WAILING OF MONSTROUS, INHUMAN FORMS.

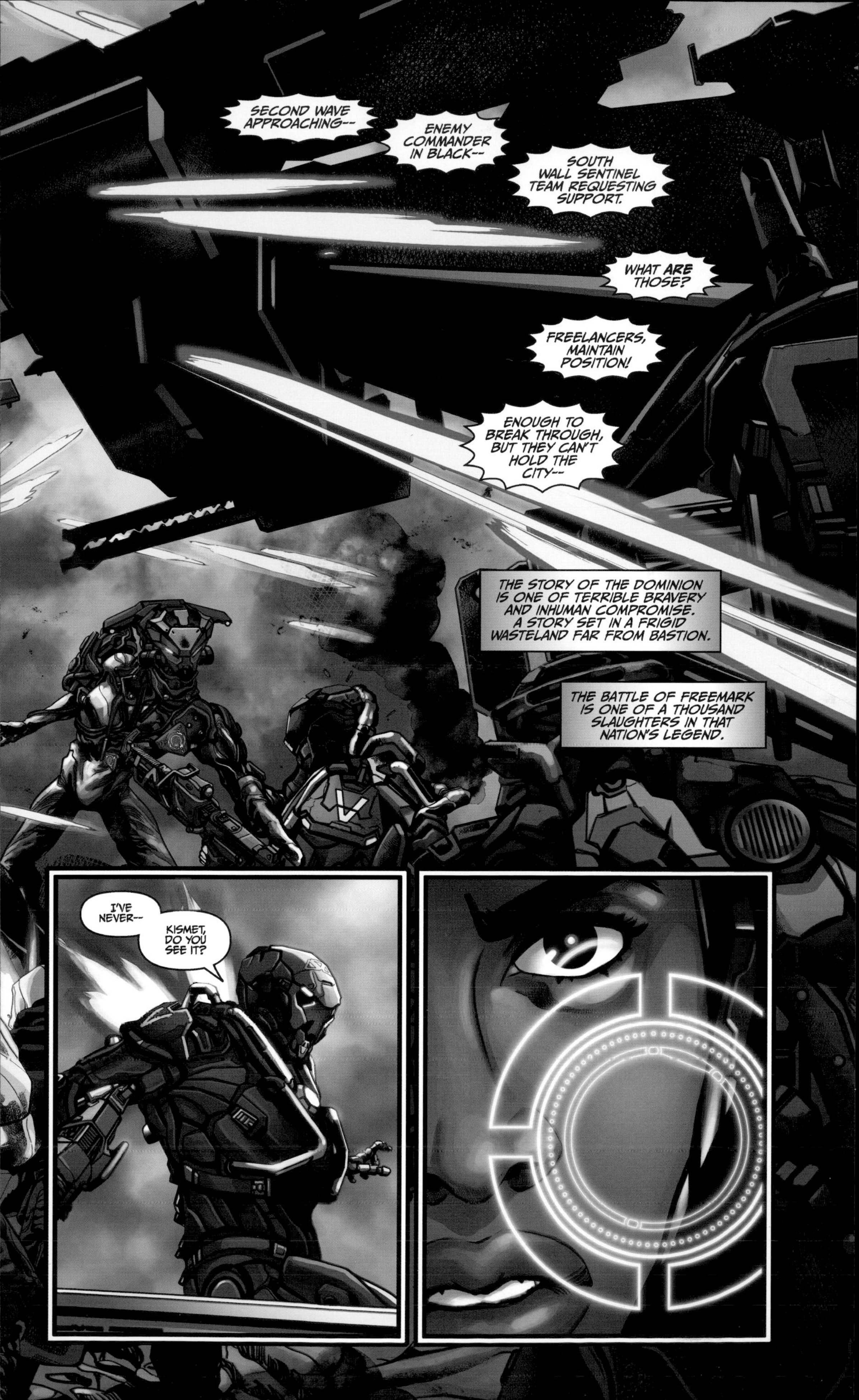
SECOND WAVE APPROACHING--
ENEMY COMMANDER IN BLACK--
SOUTH WALL SENTINEL TEAM REQUESTING SUPPORT.
WHAT ARE THOSE?
FREELANCERS, MAINTAIN POSITION!
ENOUGH TO BREAK THROUGH, BUT THEY CAN'T HOLD THE CITY--
THE STORY OF THE DOMINION IS ONE OF TERRIBLE BRAVERY AND INHUMAN COMPROMISE. A STORY SET IN A FRIGID WASTELAND FAR FROM BASTION.
THE BATTLE OF FREEMARK IS ONE OF A THOUSAND SLAUGHTERS IN THAT NATION'S LEGEND.
I'VE NEVER--
KISMET, DO YOU SEE IT?

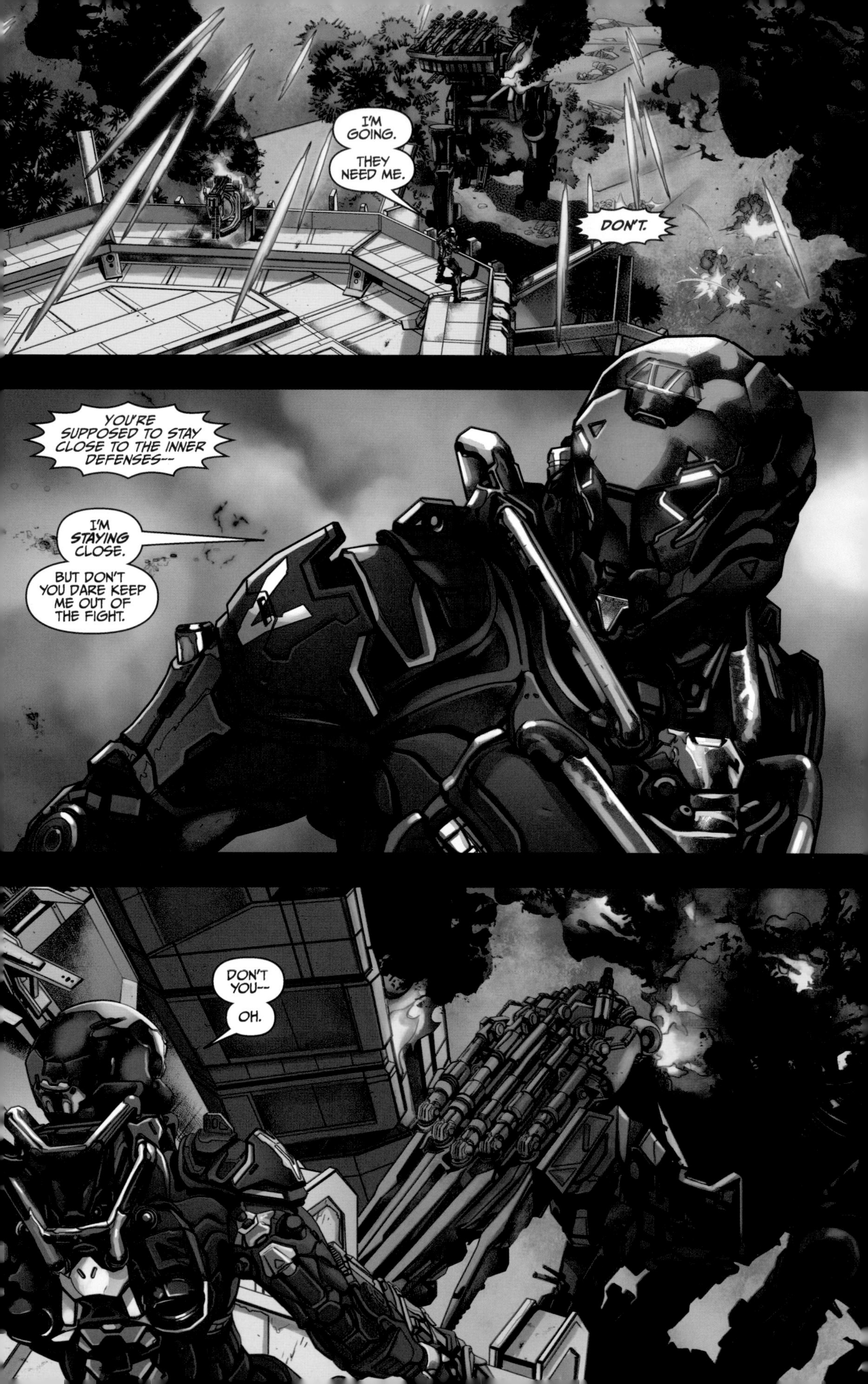
I'M GOING.
THEY NEED ME.
DON'T.
YOU'RE SUPPOSED TO STAY CLOSE TO THE INNER DEFENSES--
I'M STAYING CLOSE.
BUT DON'T YOU DARE KEEP ME OUT OF THE FIGHT.
DON'T YOU--
OH.

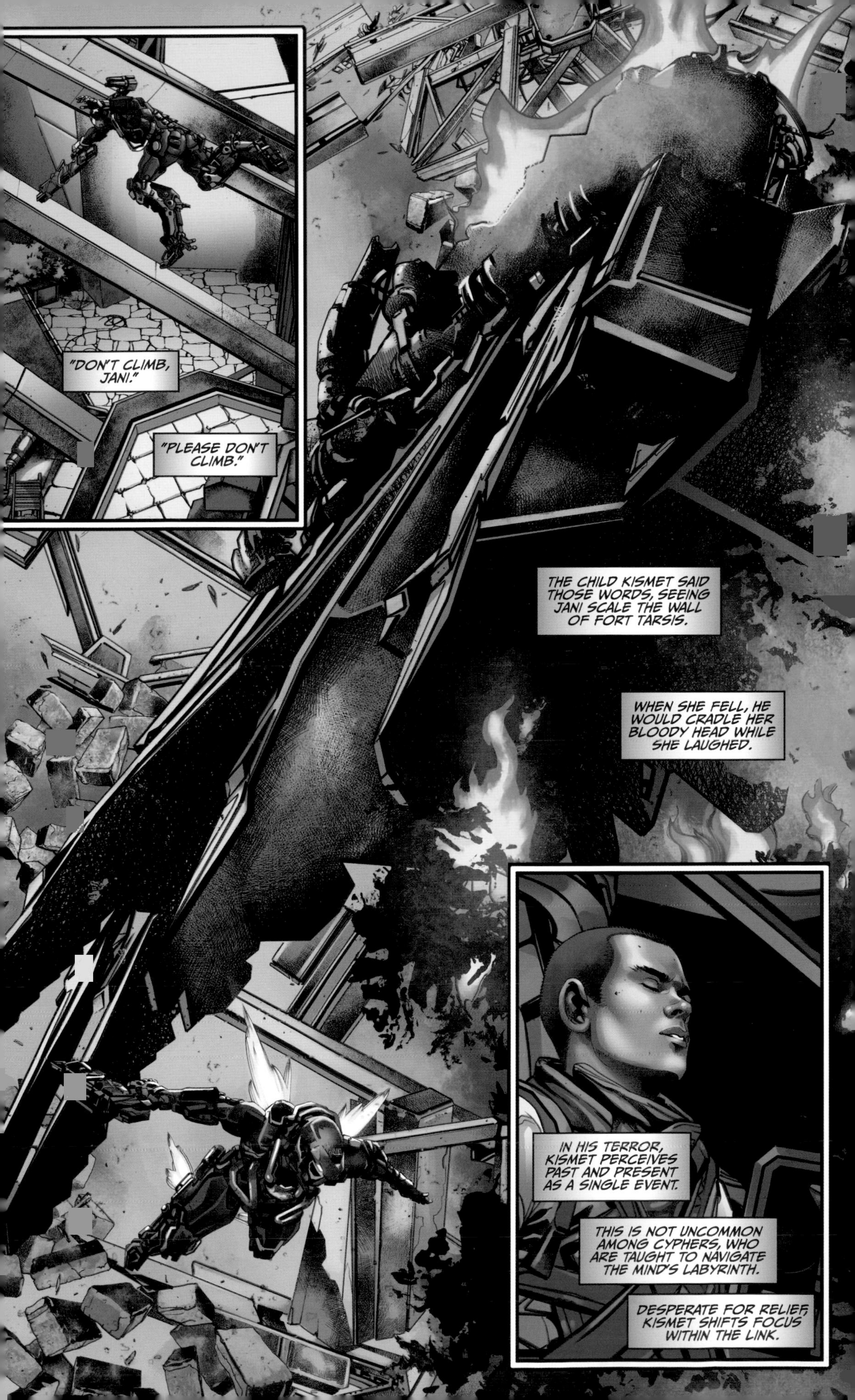

"DON'T CLIMB, JANI."
"PLEASE DON'T CLIMB."
THE CHILD KISMET SAID THOSE WORDS, SEEING JANI SCALE THE WALL OF FORT TARSIS.
WHEN SHE FELL, HE WOULD CRADLE HER BLOODY HEAD WHILE SHE LAUGHED.
IN HIS TERROR, KISMET PERCEIVES PAST AND PRESENT AS A SINGLE EVENT.
THIS IS NOT UNCOMMON AMONG CYPHERS, WHO ARE TAUGHT TO NAVIGATE THE MIND'S LABYRINTH.
DESPERATE FOR RELIEF, KISMET SHIFTS FOCUS WITHIN THE LINK.

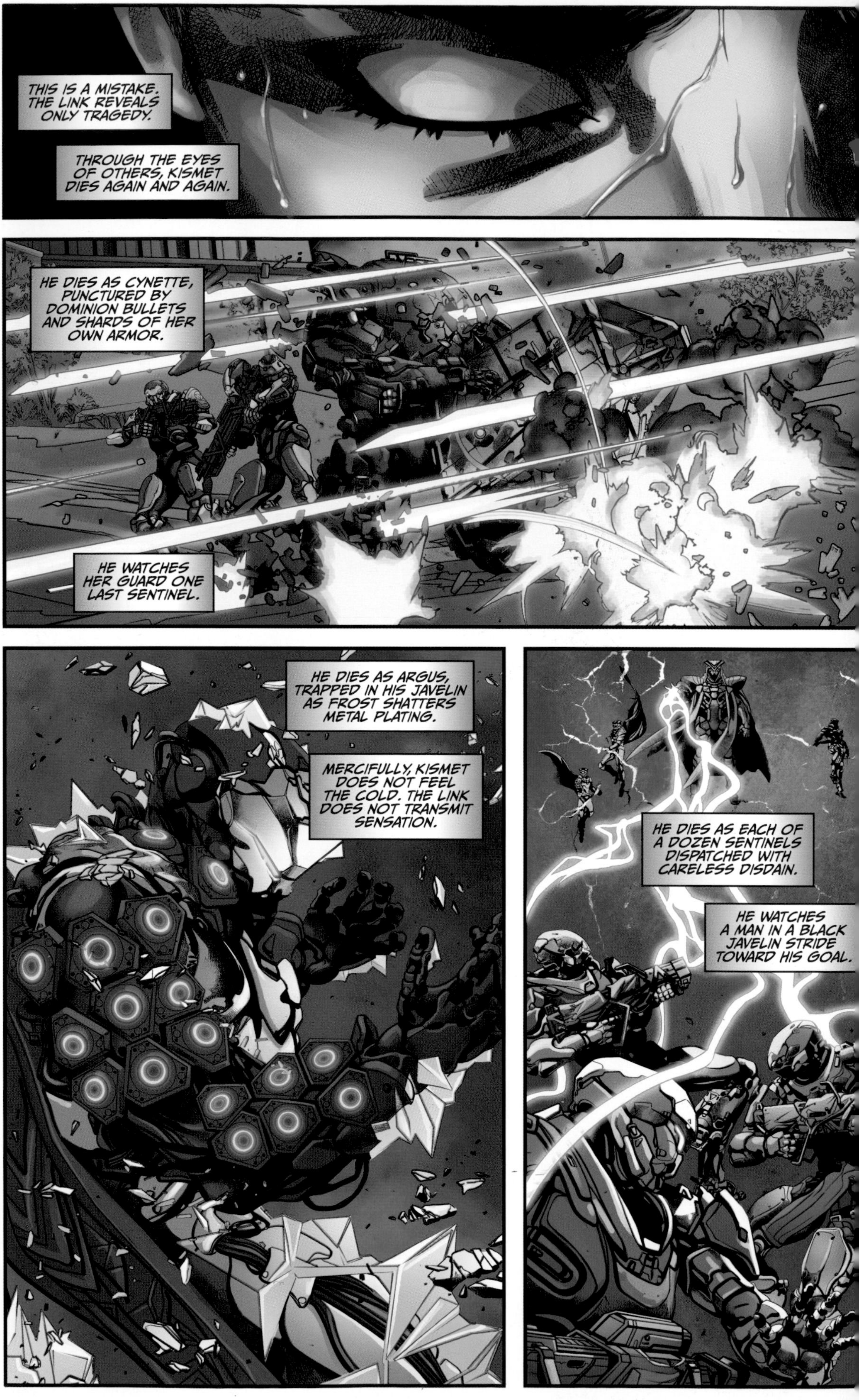
THIS IS A MISTAKE. THE LINK REVEALS ONLY TRAGEDY.
THROUGH THE EYES OF OTHERS, KISMET DIES AGAIN AND AGAIN.
HE DIES AS CYNETTE, PUNCTURED BY DOMINION BULLETS AND SHARDS OF HER OWN ARMOR.
HE WATCHES HER GUARD ONE LAST SENTINEL.
HE DIES AS ARGUS, TRAPPED IN HIS JAVELIN AS FROST SHATTERS METAL PLATING.
MERCIFULLY, KISMET DOES NOT FEEL THE COLD. THE LINK DOES NOT TRANSMIT SENSATION.
HE DIES AS EACH OF A DOZEN SENTINELS DISPATCHED WITH CARELESS DISDAIN.
HE WATCHES A MAN IN A BLACK JAVELIN STRIDE TOWARD HIS GOAL.

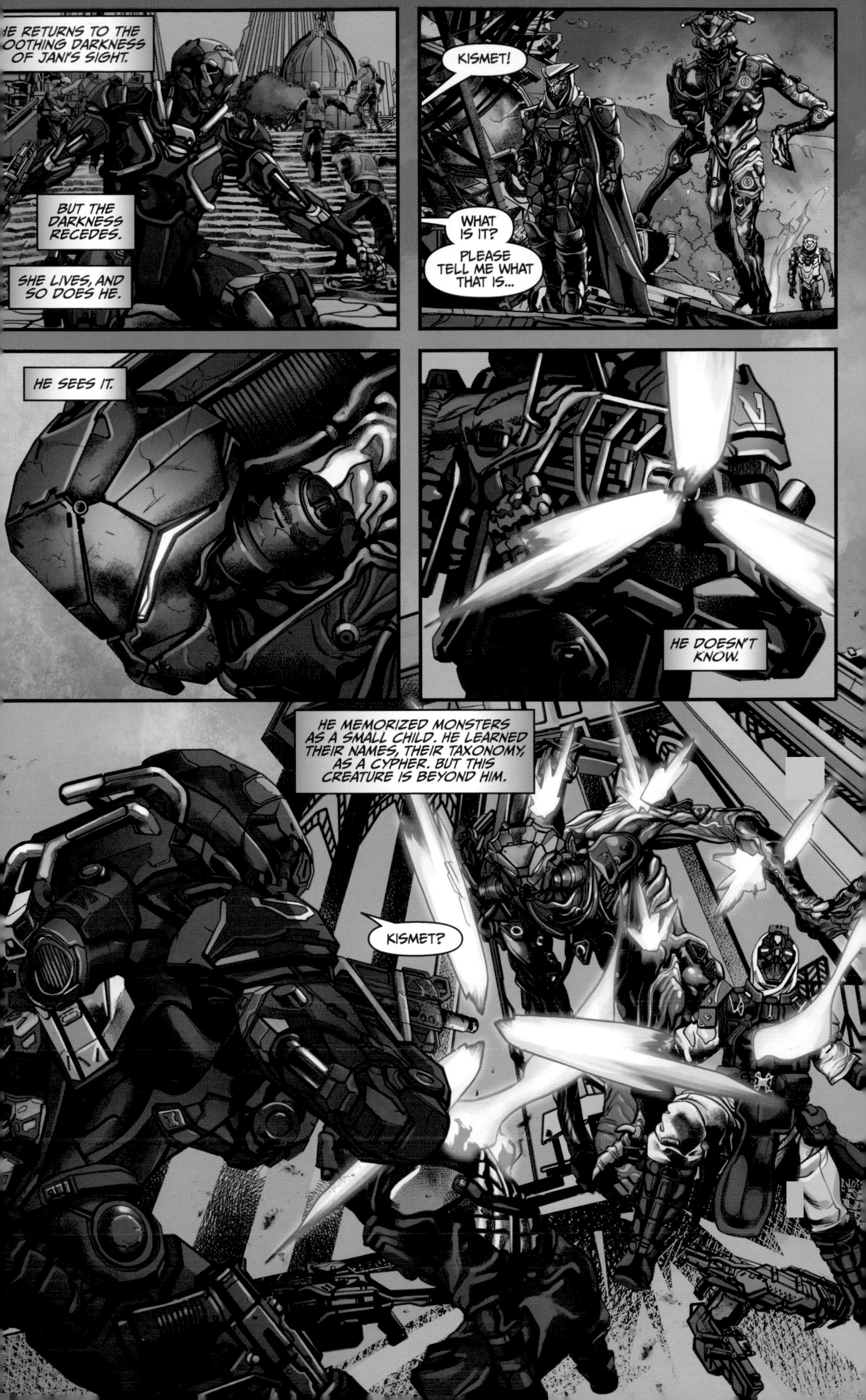
HE RETURNS TO THE SOOTHING DARKNESS OF JANI'S SIGHT.
BUT THE DARKNESS RECEDES.
SHE LIVES, AND SO DOES HE.
KISMET!
WHAT IS IT?
PLEASE TELL ME WHAT THAT IS...
HE SEES IT.
HE DOESN'T KNOW.
HE MEMORIZED MONSTERS AS A SMALL CHILD. HE LEARNED THEIR NAMES, THEIR TAXONOMY, AS A CYPHER. BUT THIS CREATURE IS BEYOND HIM.
KISMET?

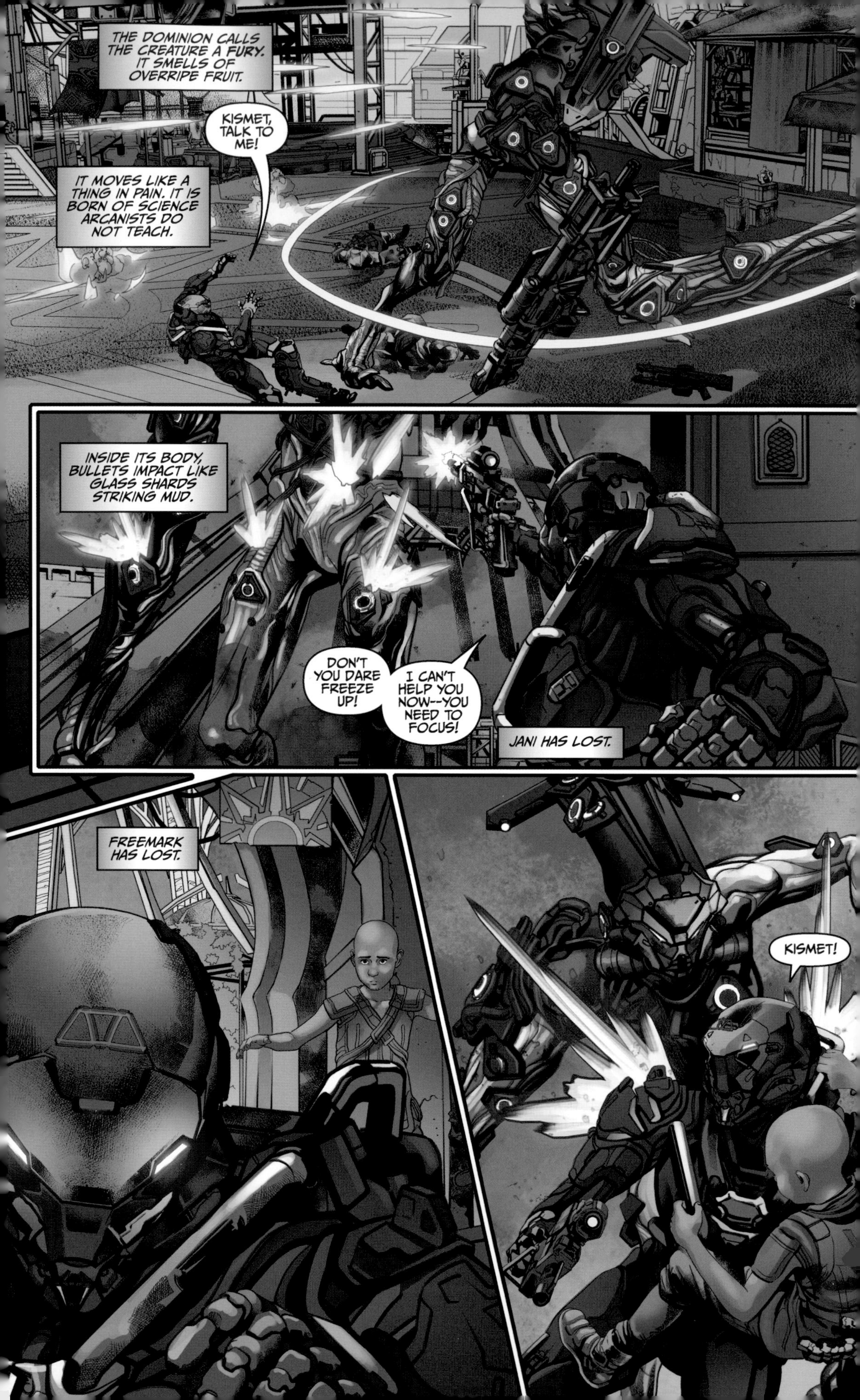
THE DOMINION CALLS THE CREATURE A FURY. IT SMELLS OF OVERRIPE FRUIT.
KISMET, TALK TO ME!
IT MOVES LIKE A THING IN PAIN. IT IS BORN OF SCIENCE ARCANISTS DO NOT TEACH.
INSIDE ITS BODY, BULLETS IMPACT LIKE GLASS SHARDS STRIKING MUD.
DON'T YOU DARE FREEZE UP!
I CAN'T HELP YOU NOW--YOU NEED TO FOCUS!
JANI HAS LOST.
FREEMARK HAS LOST.
KISMET!

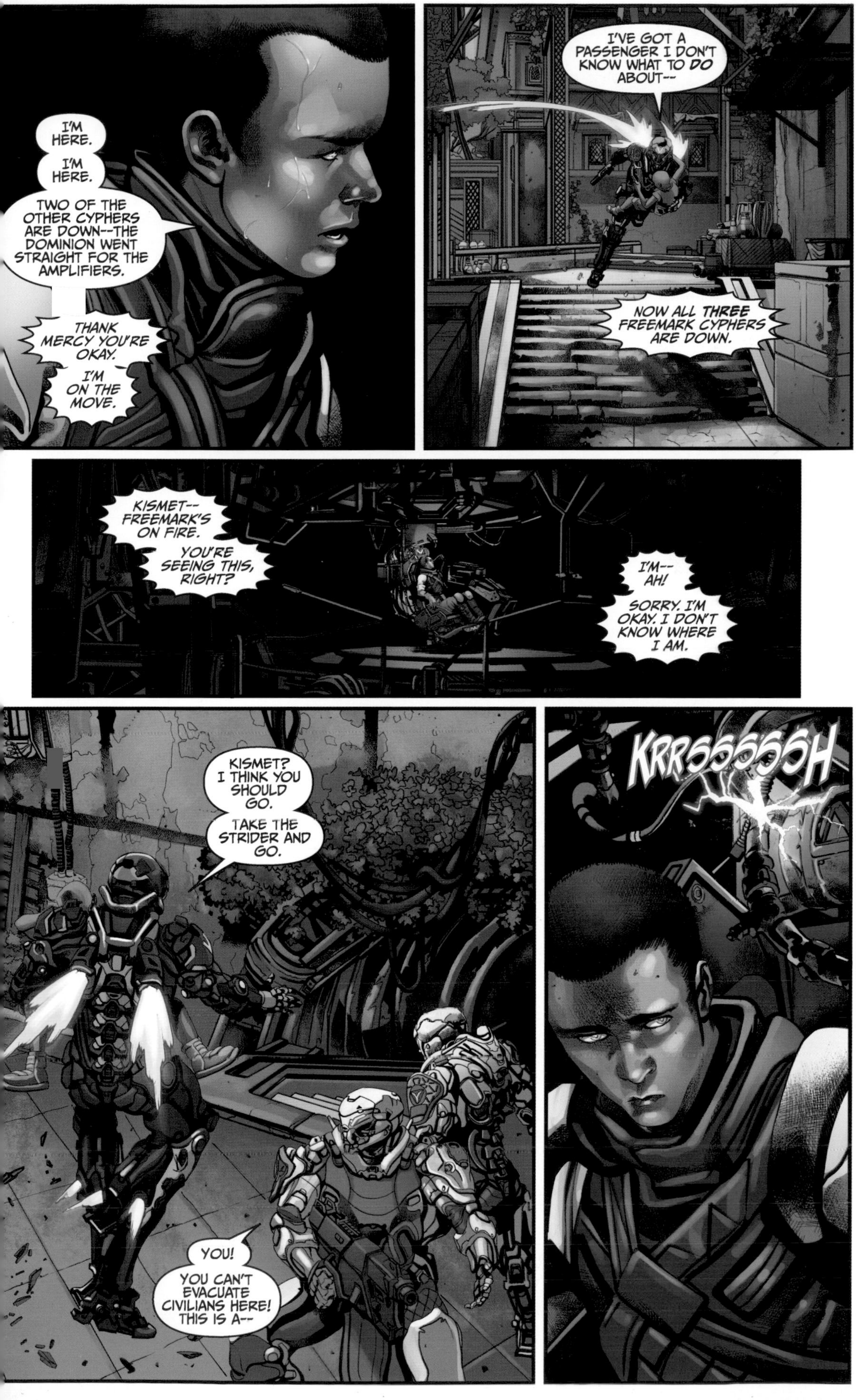
I'M HERE.
I'M HERE.
TWO OF THE OTHER CYPHERS ARE DOWN--THE DOMINION WENT STRAIGHT FOR THE AMPLIFIERS.
THANK MERCY YOU'RE OKAY.
I'M ON THE MOVE.
I'VE GOT A PASSENGER I DON'T KNOW WHAT TO DO ABOUT--
NOW ALL THREE FREEMARK CYPHERS ARE DOWN.
KISMET-- FREEMARK'S ON FIRE.
YOU'RE SEEING THIS, RIGHT?
I'M-- AH!
SORRY. I'M OKAY. I DON'T KNOW WHERE I AM.
KISMET? I THINK YOU SHOULD GO.
TAKE THE STRIDER AND GO.
YOU!
YOU CAN'T EVACUATE CIVILIANS HERE! THIS IS A--
KRRSSSSSH

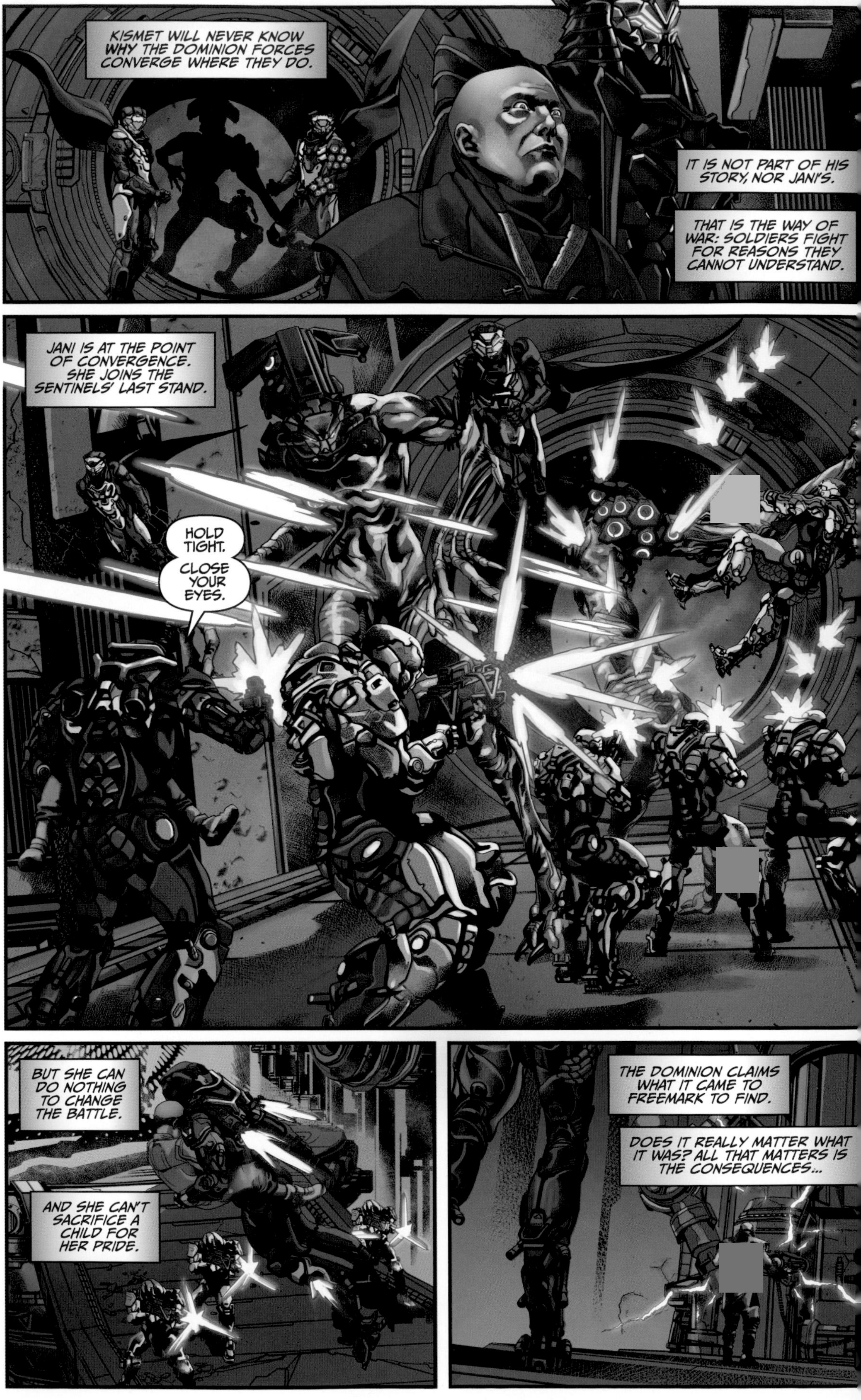
KISMET WILL NEVER KNOW WHY THE DOMINION FORCES CONVERGE WHERE THEY DO.
IT IS NOT PART OF HIS STORY, NOR JANI'S.
THAT IS THE WAY OF WAR: SOLDIERS FIGHT FOR REASONS THEY CANNOT UNDERSTAND.
JANI IS AT THE POINT OF CONVERGENCE. SHE JOINS THE SENTINELS' LAST STAND.
HOLD TIGHT.
CLOSE YOUR EYES.
BUT SHE CAN DO NOTHING TO CHANGE THE BATTLE.
AND SHE CAN'T SACRIFICE A CHILD FOR HER PRIDE.
THE DOMINION CLAIMS WHAT IT CAME TO FREEMARK TO FIND.
DOES IT REALLY MATTER WHAT IT WAS? ALL THAT MATTERS IS THE CONSEQUENCES...

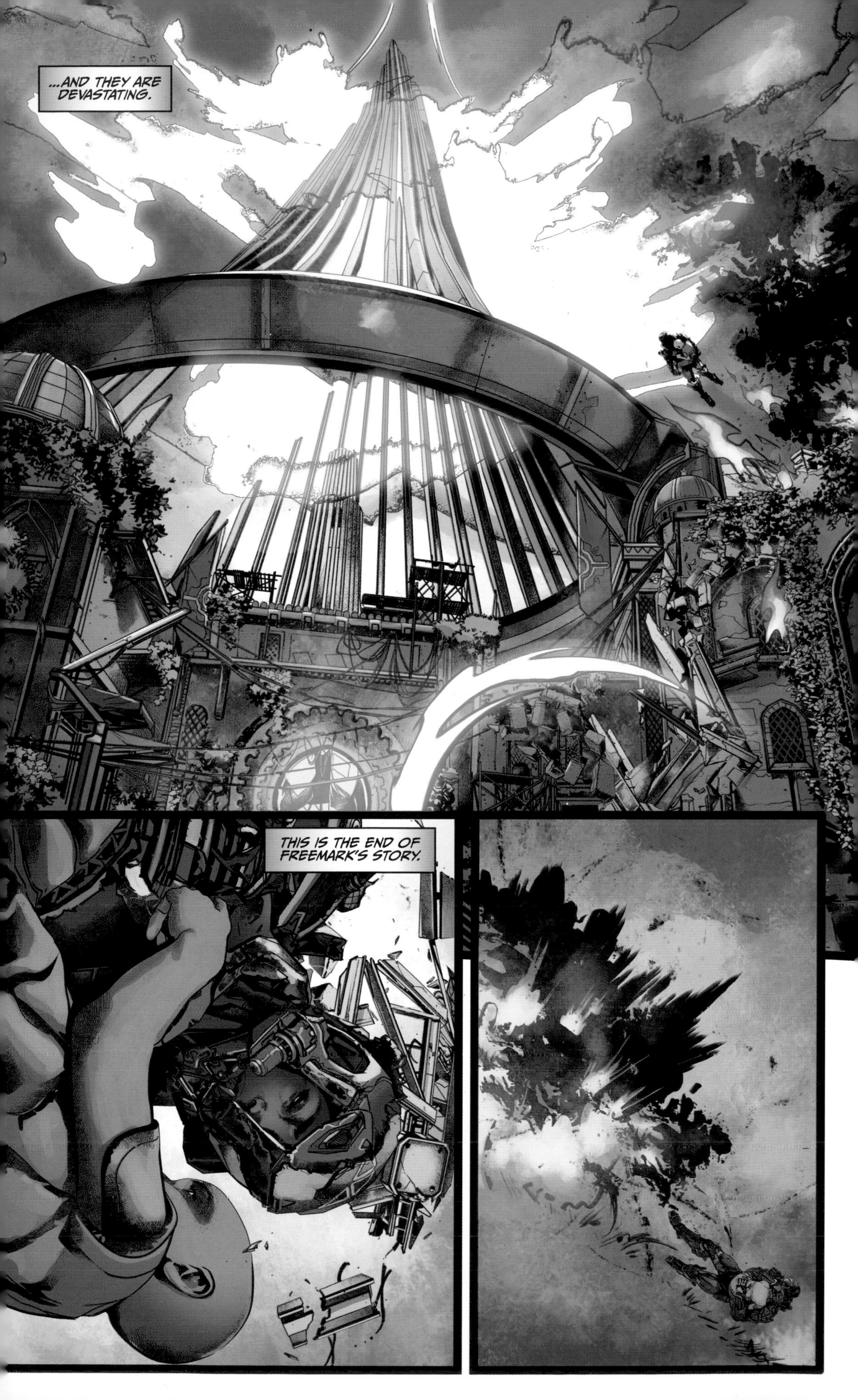
...AND THEY ARE DEVASTATING.
THIS IS THE END OF FREEMARK'S STORY.

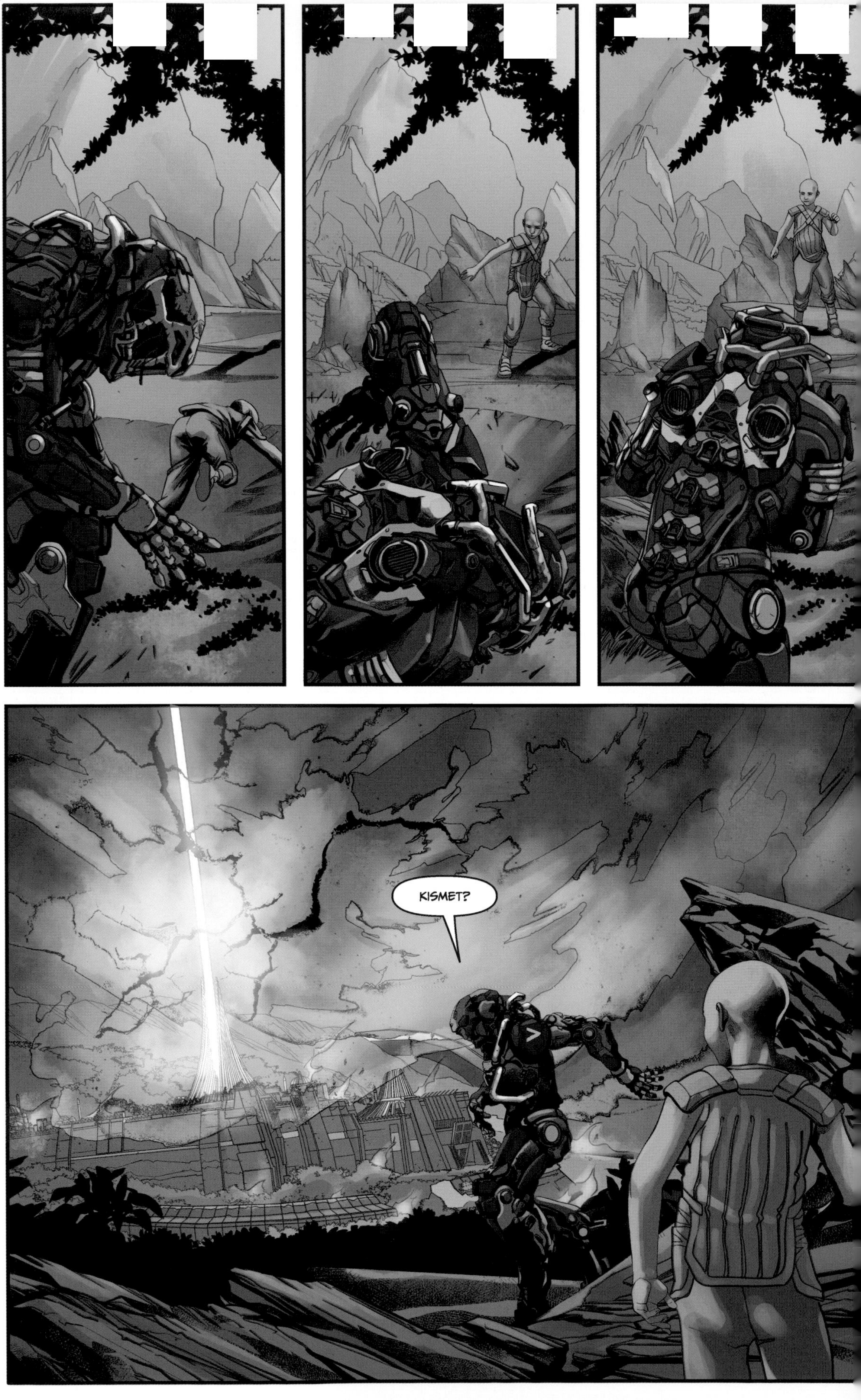
KISMET?

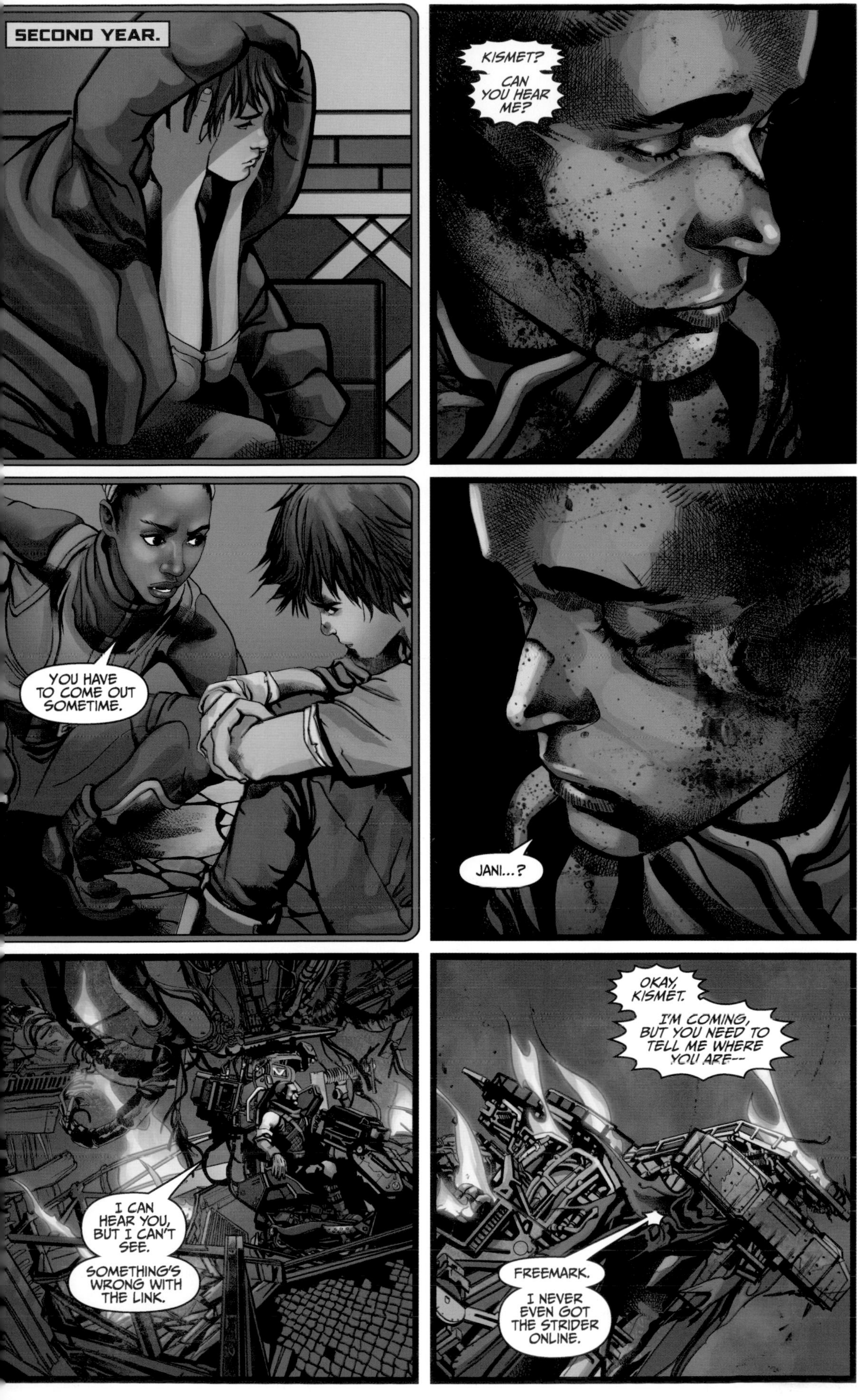
SECOND YEAR.
KISMET? CAN YOU HEAR ME?
YOU HAVE TO COME OUT SOMETIME.
JANI...?
I CAN HEAR YOU, BUT I CAN'T SEE.
SOMETHING'S WRONG WITH THE LINK.
OKAY, KISMET.
I'M COMING, BUT YOU NEED TO TELL ME WHERE YOU ARE--
FREEMARK.
I NEVER EVEN GOT THE STRIDER ONLINE.

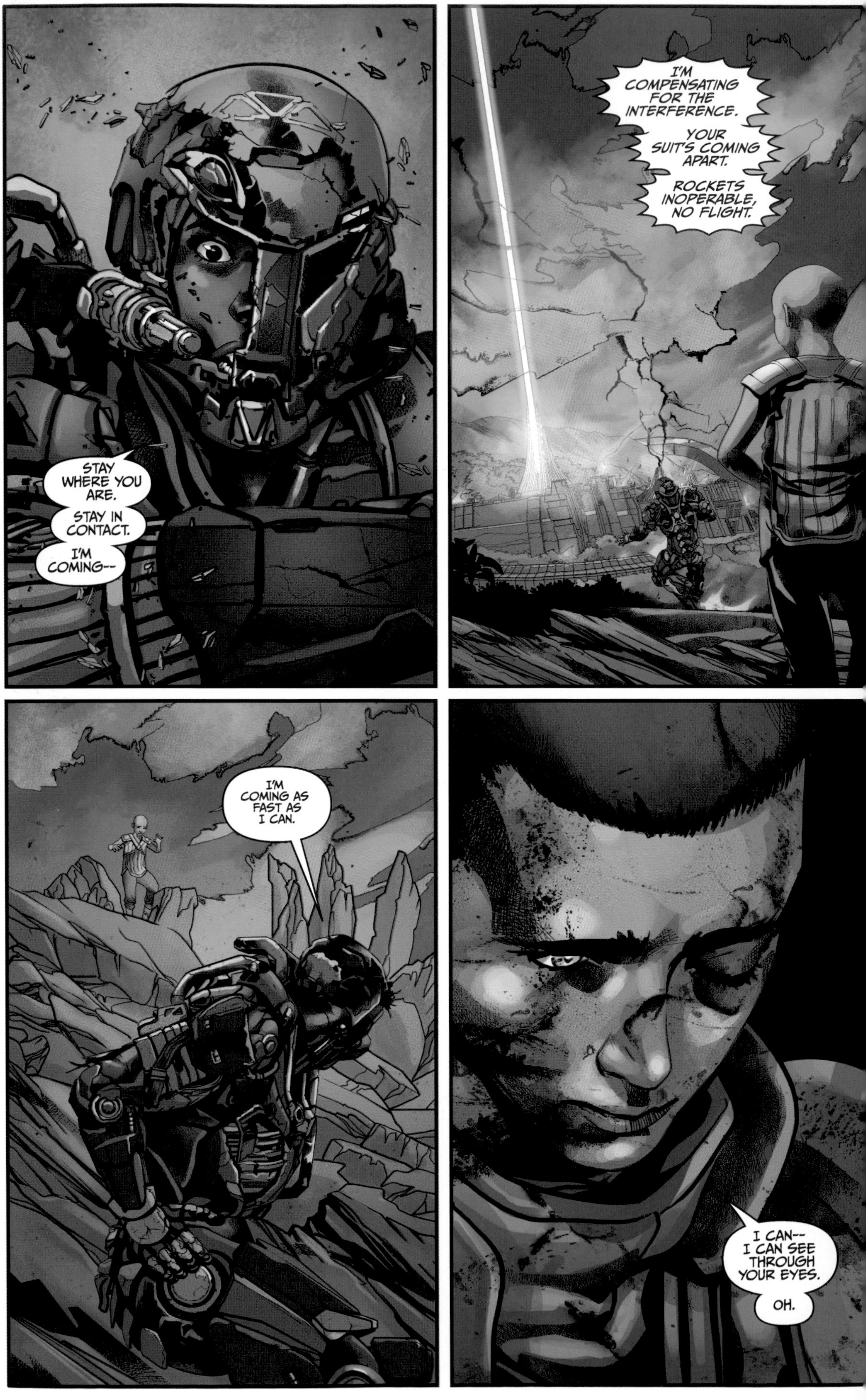
STAY WHERE YOU ARE.
STAY IN CONTACT.
I'M COMING--
I'M COMPENSATING FOR THE INTERFERENCE.
YOUR SUIT'S COMING APART.
ROCKETS INOPERABLE, NO FLIGHT.
I'M COMING AS FAST AS I CAN.
I CAN-- I CAN SEE THROUGH YOUR EYES.
OH.

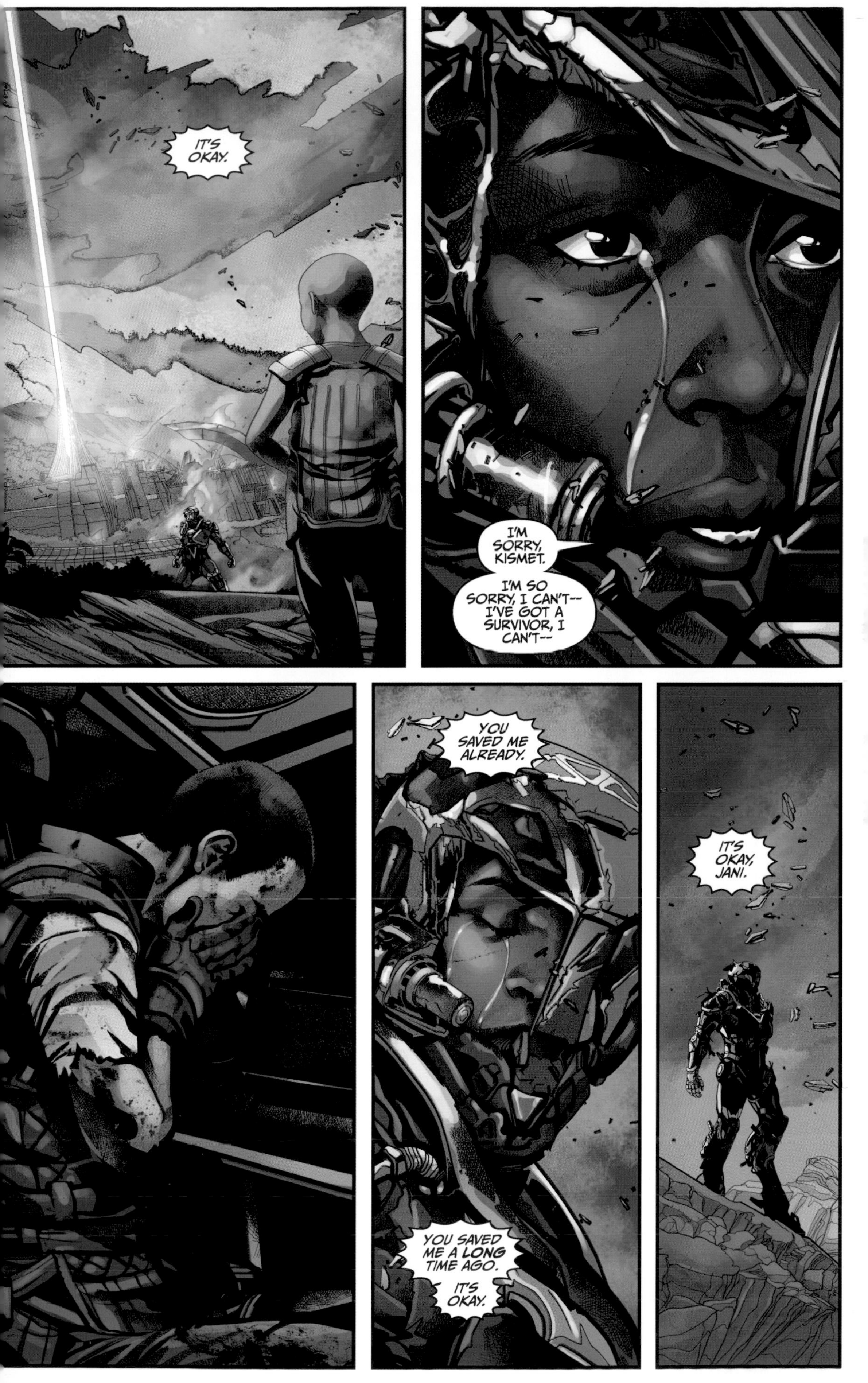
IT'S OKAY.
I'M SORRY, KISMET.
I'M SO SORRY, I CAN'T-- I'VE GOT A SURVIVOR, I CAN'T--
YOU SAVED ME ALREADY.
YOU SAVED ME A LONG TIME AGO.
IT'S OKAY.
IT'S OKAY, JANI.

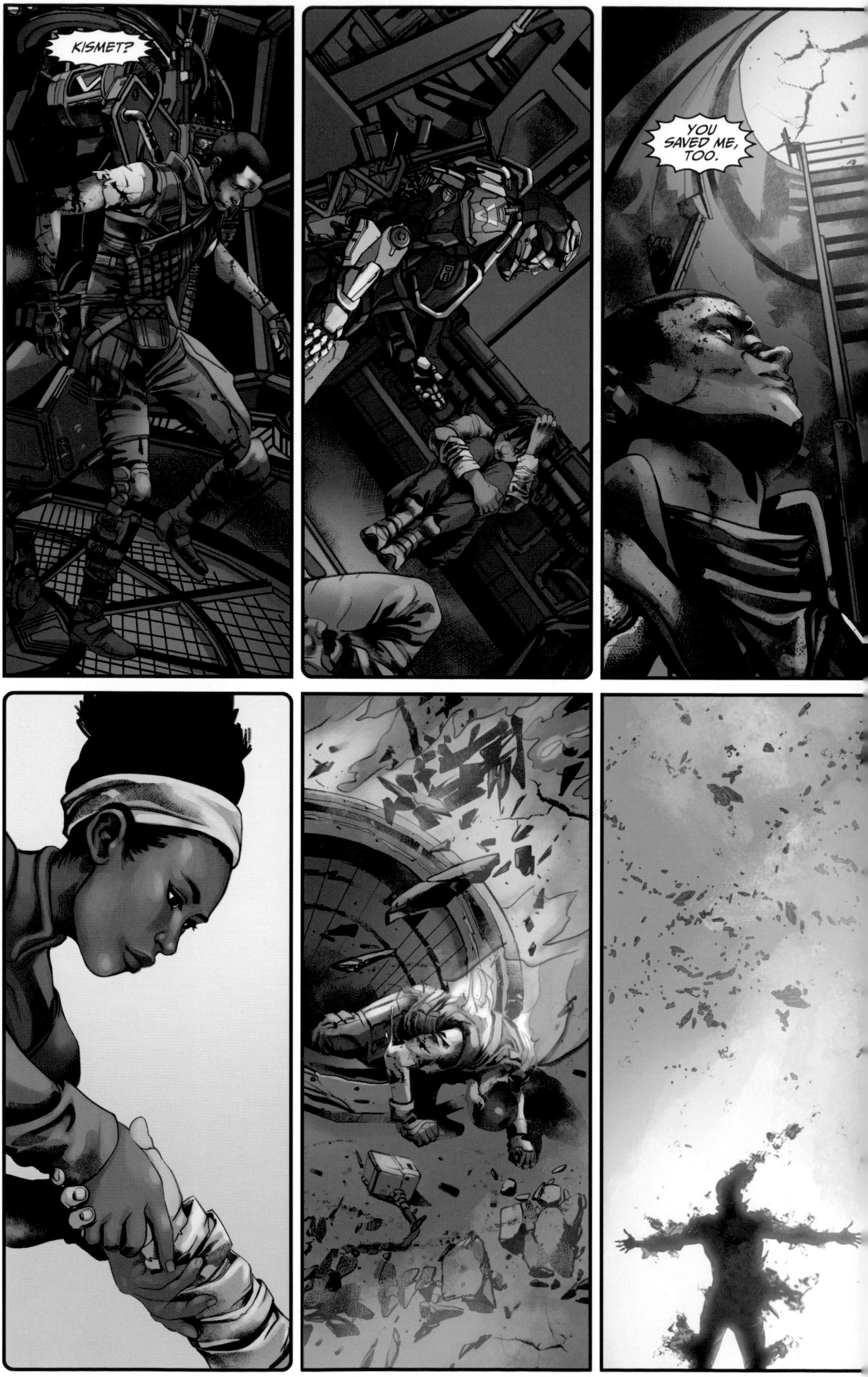
KISMET?
YOU SAVED ME, TOO.

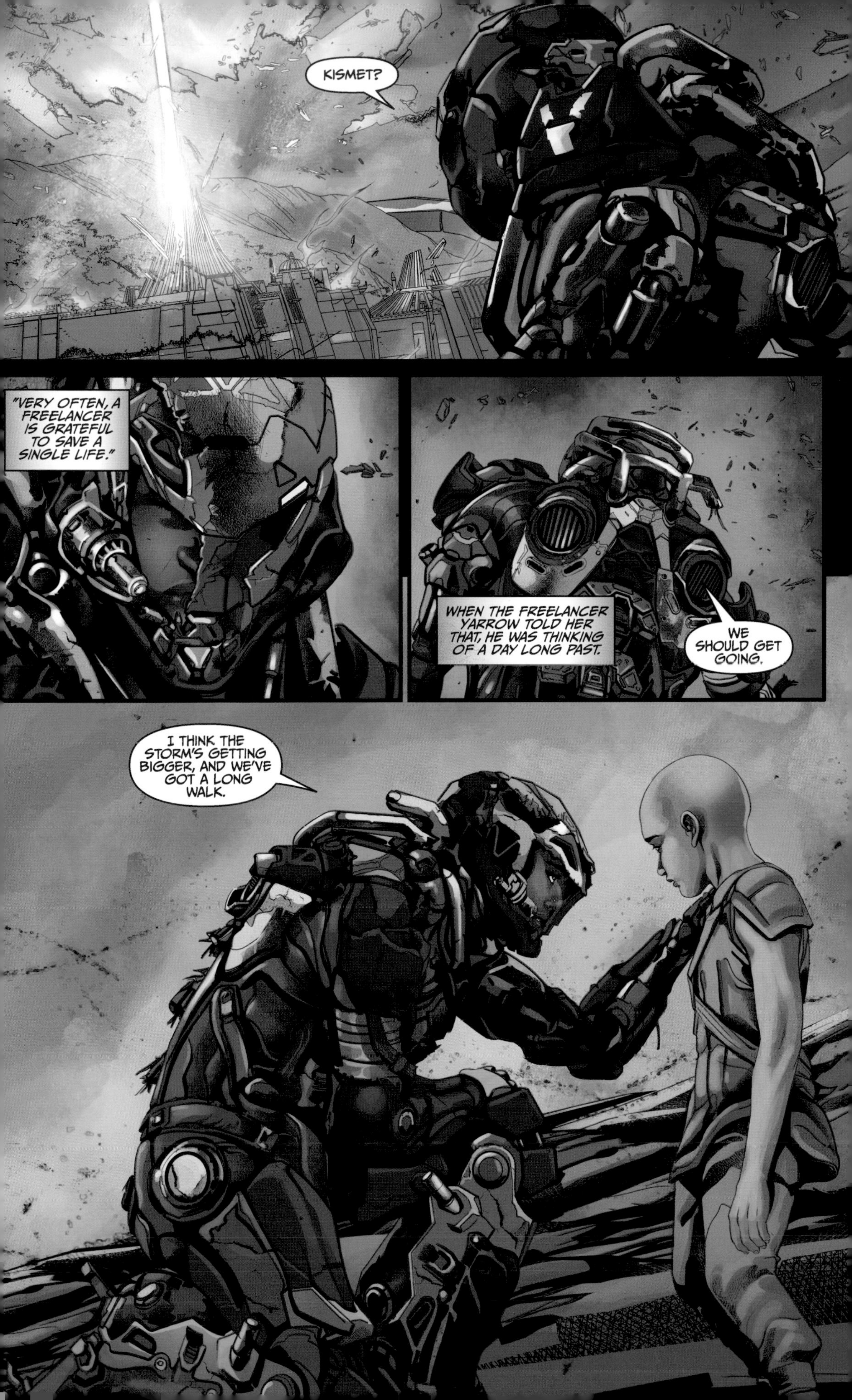
KISMET?
"VERY OFTEN, A FREELANCER IS GRATEFUL TO SAVE A SINGLE LIFE."
WHEN THE FREELANCER YARROW TOLD HER THAT, HE WAS THINKING OF A DAY LONG PAST.
WE SHOULD GET GOING.
I THINK THE STORM'S GETTING BIGGER, AND WE'VE GOT A LONG WALK.

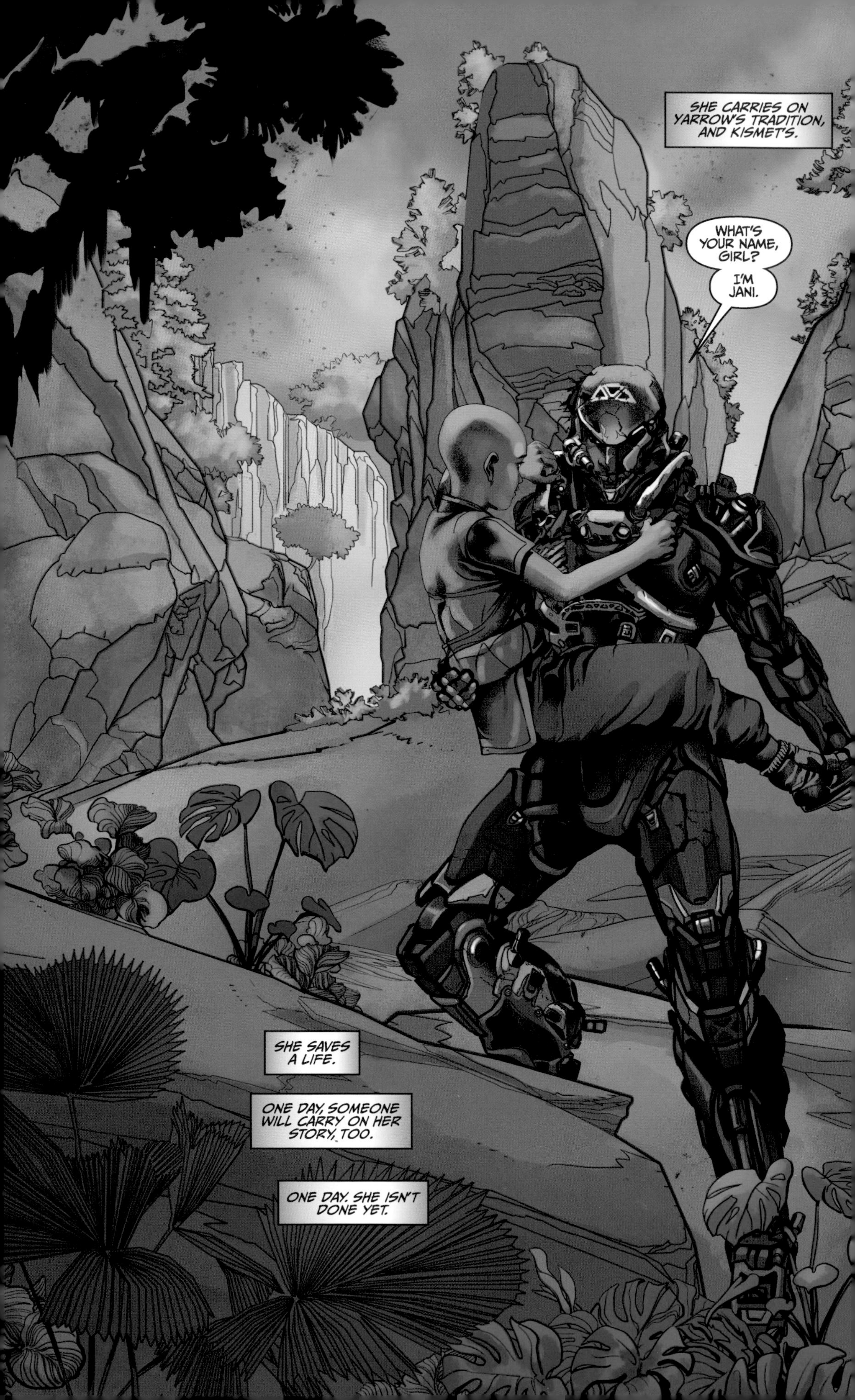
SHE CARRIES ON YARROW'S TRADITION, AND KISMET'S.
WHAT'S YOUR NAME, GIRL?
I'M JANI.
SHE SAVES A LIFE.
ONE DAY, SOMEONE WILL CARRY ON HER STORY, TOO.
ONE DAY. SHE ISN'T DONE YET.

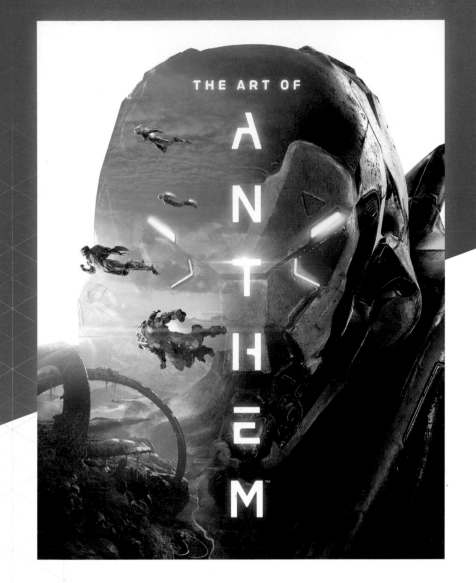

THE ART OF
ANTHEM™

Hundreds of pieces of art with commentary detailing the creation of
BioWare's groundbreaking epic in an expertly designed hardcover volume!

From the studio behind the hit franchises *Dragon Age* and *Mass Effect* comes the thrilling world of *Anthem*. Dark Horse Books
and BioWare are proud to present *The Art of Anthem*, showcasing the grandeur and beauty of this dangerous new world.

Filled with behind-the-scenes looks at four years of game production, original concept art, and exclusive commentary from
developers, *The Art of Anthem* is a fantastic addition to any gamer fan's bookshelf!

ISBN 978-1-50670-701-3 $39.99

△△△

EXPLORE THE MASS EFFECT UNIVERSE WITH DARK HORSE!

Created in close collaboration with BioWare and the writers and artists of the games, Dark Horse's *Mass Effect* graphic novels are essential companions to gaming's deepest universe!

MASS EFFECT
OMNIBUS
VOLUME 1

MASS EFFECT OMNIBUS VOLUME 1
ISBN 978-1-50670-276-6 | **$24.99**

MASS EFFECT
OMNIBUS
VOLUME 2

MASS EFFECT OMNIBUS VOLUME 2
ISBN 978-1-50670-277-3 | **$24.99**

1
REDEMPTION
EVOLUTION
INVASION
HOMEWORLDS
MASS EFFECT
MAC WALTERS OMAR FRANCIA JOHN JACKSON MILLER

MASS EFFECT LIBRARY EDITION VOLUME 1
ISBN 978-1-61655-111-7 | **$59.99**

MASS EFFECT LIBRARY EDITION VOLUME 2
ISBN 978-1-61655-636-5 | **$49.99**

THE ART OF THE
MASS EFFECT
UNIVERSE
INTRODUCTIONS BY
CASEY HUDSON AND DEREK WATTS

THE ART OF THE MASS EFFECT UNIVERSE
ISBN 978-1-59582-768-5 | **$39.99**

AVAILABLE AT YOUR LOCAL COMICS SHOP OR BOOKSTORE!
To find a comics shop in your area, visit comicshoplocator.com
For more information or to order direct: • On the web: DarkHorse.com
• Email: mailorder@darkhorse.com • Phone: 1-800-862-0052 Mon.–Fri. 9 AM to 5 PM Pacific Time.

DarkHorse.com
MassEffect.com

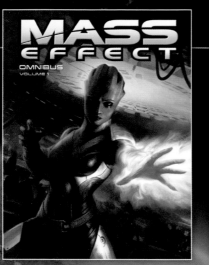

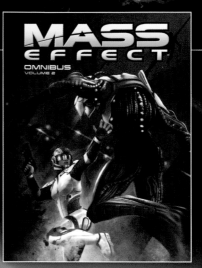

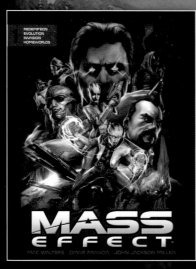

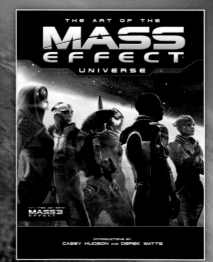